SKIP THE LINE

Also by James Altucher

Choose Yourself!
Reinvent Yourself
The Power of No

SKIP THE LINE

THE 10,000 EXPERIMENTS RULE AND OTHER SURPRISING ADVICE FOR REACHING YOUR GOALS

JAMES ALTUCHER

PAPL DISCARDED

HARPER
BUSINESS

An Imprint of HarperCollinsPublishers

HarperCollins books may be purchased for educational, business, or sales promotional use. For information, please email the Special Markets Department at SPsales@harpercollins.com.

FIRST EDITION

Designed by Kyle O'Brien

Library of Congress Cataloging-in-Publication Data
Names: Altucher, James, author.
Title: Skip the line : the 10,000 experiments rule and other surprising advice for reaching your goals / James Altucher.
Description: First edition. | New York, NY : Harper Business, an Imprint of HarperCollinsPublishers, [2021]
Identifiers: LCCN 2020039733 (print) | LCCN 2020039734 (ebook) | ISBN 9780062998927 (hardcover) | ISBN 9780062998934 (ebook)
Subjects: LCSH: Entrepreneurship. | Self-realization. | Success.
Classification: LCC HB615 .A68198 2021 (print) | LCC HB615 (ebook) | DDC 650.1—dc23
LC record available at https://lccn.loc.gov/2020039733
LC ebook record available at https://lccn.loc.gov/2020039734

21 22 23 24 25 LSC 10 9 8 7 6 5 4 3 2 1

Dedicated to Robyn Altucher:

I'm so glad I met you in time to be quarantined with you.

CONTENTS

SKIP THE LINE

INTRODUCTION

"You can't do that!"

She's the head of marketing at HBO. I'm walking toward the CEO's office. It's 1995. The CEO is my boss's boss's boss's boss's boss.

My official title at HBO is junior analyst software developer. If I worked hard, I'd get a promotion to senior analyst software developer.

Cindy says, "You can't just walk into the CEO's office and tell him an idea! Do you know how many people have ideas for a show who have been in this business for decades? And you can't just go over your boss's head. You can't skip the line!"

But I want to change my life. I'm unhappy. My career feels stagnant. I'm not interested in being a junior analyst . . . whatever. Being comfortable in my nice little cubicle. Six feet by six feet. Even in a jail, prisoners often have an eight-by-eight cell. They have their own bathroom. I don't like going to the bathroom and thinking my boss might be in the stall next to me. I've ruined my stomach forever by holding it in until work is over.

Can I skip the line?

"I'm going to try," I say. "What can I lose?"

"You can lose your job," she says. "Nobody does this."

But I want to. I want to skip the line. I'm not taking an easy shortcut. My idea is good. Who made the rules that you can't skip the line?

I go to the CEO's office . . .

◆ ◆ ◆

Twenty-five years later, a pandemic shuts down the planet. Forty million people in the United States file for unemployment. The world feels over. People start to riot. There are protests everywhere. As the economy reopens, as the dust starts to clear, we can see the results: Many businesses are not coming back. Many industries are upside down. Many people are lost in this new world.

The ability to change, to find your passion, to get good at it, to make money from it, to feed your family, to be excited . . . *again*, to want that excitement about getting up in the morning—this has never been more important. They never taught us the "skip the line" skills in school. They never told us that the world can suddenly become very terrifying unless we know how to live in the land of not-knowing.

Maybe I'll change my passion again. And again. It's never too late. Everyone is walking around shaken with some kind of societal PTSD. I want to change, people say. I've always wanted to do X but I thought I had to do Y. From birth we're told which holidays to celebrate, which schools to go to, which promotions to aim for, which awards to strive for. I kept believing this until I was on the floor, flirting with the worst, no optimism left.

The time to learn to skip the line is now. But the time to learn to skip the line was always now; we just forgot that.

◆ ◆ ◆

I lived four blocks from the World Trade Center on 9/11.

It was such a beautiful morning, around 8:30 a.m., September 11, 2001. The markets had been down for several days in a row and I had made a big bet the night before that the markets would bounce back.

At that moment, the stock market looked like it would open up big, and I was excited to make money.

I'm having breakfast at the Dean & DeLuca on the bottom floor of One World Trade Center. Then my business partner, Dan, and I start walking back toward my apartment.

Dan turns to me and says, "Is the president coming in today?" He points up in front of us to a low-flying jet cutting through the sky right toward us.

A second later—a microsecond—a second that will never repeat, everyone on the street instinctively ducks. My eyes open. I see the plane scream straight into the building, accompanied by the loudest sound ever—imagine a god opening up the door of a giant attic.

Dan and I run to the nearest fire station. We want to help. I tell them. One guy throws us two suits to wear inside the buildings. "Put these on." And then he asks, "Are you guys firefighters?"

"No, but we can help."

"Forget it. You have to be firefighters." And he and the other guys in the fire station put on their suits, get in the truck, turn on the siren, and leave. Many died less than an hour later as the buildings crashed in on them.

We go back toward the smoking buildings. People are throwing themselves off the top. From a distance they look like black squiggles twisting in the air. Up closer you see the more familiar outlines of bodies. Then the buildings start to shake, and then tumble, sending up enormous amounts of smoke and blackness. We run back to my apartment. The black cloud covers the entire building.

My little daughter had peed on the floor. Everyone is scared. People who had gathered in my apartment are crying. Everyone feels powerless. Nobody knows what to do. Announcements blasted over a bullhorn tell us to leave the area, but we don't. Is it safer outside or inside?

we wonder. Our windows are pitch-black, all the dust and destruction trying to pound their way into the apartment. We stay up all night, taking turns listening to the radio, and the next day, Part Two of everyone's lives begins.

A few months later, I'm dead broke from day-trading. I knew nothing about day-trading, but I had gambled away millions of dollars. At night, I dream of enormous tidal waves sweeping over Manhattan, and I wake the moment I realize in the dream that I can't run fast enough to escape.

I want to sell my house. I've already lowered the price three times, but there are no buyers. Every day I call the broker. He says, "Move the price down again." I don't want to. I do it anyway.

More waiting.

I look in my bank account again: $143. How did this happen? I think I'm smart, but I've been the biggest idiot. I cry. What do I do?

I call my wife. I'm supposed to get something from the store, but in my panic after I saw my bank account I totally forgot what I'm supposed to get.

I go to a payphone (New York City still had them at the time) and start dialing. I don't hear a dial tone. I press the keys. No sounds. I feel something against my ear. I pull the phone away but it's sticky and grabbing on to my hair.

The phone is covered in shit. Human shit? Dog shit? I don't know. And now it's all over my hands and hair. When I was eight years old and thought my future would take me from success to success, I never would've predicted this moment. I drop the phone quickly. I yell out but people keep walking by.

Dead broke, shit in my hair, and I forgot what I'm supposed to get at the store.

That night I go to my neighbor. I'm desperate.

"Do you think I can get a job investing at the fund you work for?"

He looks down, maybe a little embarrassed, and hesitates. I'm feeling like I'm going to cry again. I hate asking people for things.

He says, "You might need a little experience. Like maybe a degree in finance, or maybe you need to work at a bank or a fund for a while and start from the bottom. You know, there's a lot of people trying to get into this business. It's hard to skip the line."

I really hate when people tell me that.

I had to change. Once again I had to change. I had to change everything. I had to find something I could be obsessed about. I had to get good at it. I had to make money from it. I wanted to feed my family. And I needed to do it right away. I didn't have 10,000 hours. I needed to skip the line.

🔺 🔺 🔺

I've woken up in the middle of the night, three in the morning, many times. Opening my eyes into the dark blue. So many voices racing in my head. You feel this and you wonder, whose voices are these? They won't stop.

The lateness of the hour, the dark, the voices . . . it seems that some-how my heart has taken a wrong turn. That I ended up in someone else's nightmare, running in the maze, captured by words conjured up from a horrible part of me. I can't believe that the young boy who was once so excited to wake up and play is now trapped here in the dark blue.

When someone tells you "You can't do that!" don't assume the worst. We're all trying to calm the demons inside of us. The anxieties, the stresses. Where did everyone get these anxieties? These fears? It doesn't matter. Life is more difficult than we ever could have guessed.

It only matters that you realize this: understand that when someone tells you that you can't do something, they are trying to imprint their own goals for you onto you. It is their agenda, their truth. Not yours. You don't have to follow their goals. You don't have to give the goals they have for you any of your energy. You don't even have to convince them, because they can't be convinced. They live inside their own piece of this giant simulation. Of all the possibilities in the world that are open to them, the one where you specifically "can't" is incredibly important to these people.

Let their goals slide past you. They will walk past you, muttering to their own ghosts while you move forward toward your own goals. Hope that they will be happier somehow. But don't do more than just hope. Instead, detach from their path, their vision for you, and move toward your own possibilities.

Sometimes at three in the morning those voices come back. The many "can'ts" you've been told. When the hour is late and dark and lonely, your resistance to the agendas of others is at its weakest. The brain invites them in and the heart is not quite awake to defend.

The ideas in this book are what can wake you up. You aren't lonely in your dreams. You do have power over that darkness. One agenda that many have is A, then B, C, and D, and often they think that's the only path.

The possibilities at that moment, at the moment of greatest despair, are spread out in front of you like when a magician fans out a deck of cards. Pick a card, they say, any card.

But it is then that your heart can reach for a card and pick the one that is for you only. Even at that late hour, it's time to skip the line, to explore the universe of possibilities that nobody else even believes exists. It's late and dark and you feel powerless, but you get to pick the card, any card.

Jigoro Kano, the founder of judo, was short, 5'2", and very interested in his studies at school. His family moved around a bit after his mother passed away when he was a child. In modern words, he was a "nerd." He was frequently bullied by schoolmates much bigger than him, the sort of people who would physically say, "You can't!" and make Kano pay if he tried to move forward.

Kano learned to defeat his bigger opponents by using their own energy against them. When they were on the attack, they would have a temporary loss of equilibrium. For instance, if they lunged, then at that precise moment they would be slightly off-balance. His approach was to learn to instinctively relax his mind and body at these high-stakes moments and then use his opponent's own energy against them. "Maximum efficiency, minimum energy" was his approach.

He once said, "In short, resisting a more powerful opponent will result in your defeat, whilst adjusting to and evading your opponent's attack will cause him to lose his balance, his power will be reduced, and you will defeat him. This can apply whatever the relative values of power, thus making it possible for weaker opponents to beat significantly stronger ones."

The forces of the world will always conspire against you when you try to reach for accomplishments beyond the comfort zone, beyond the straightforward path that most people subscribe to. You will be bullied. Maybe not physically but in many other ways. When someone says, "You can't!" or appears to have hostility to you skipping the line to achieve success in your chosen field, the idea of relaxing rather than resisting, of increasing and creating energy based on the actions of others, of acting when others are off-balance, fuels many of the skip-the-line techniques described in this book.

❧ ❧ ❧

"James, James, James," Vince says, "you just started doing stand-up comedy when? Two years ago? People have been doing it for years and aren't getting the spots you are getting. You have to just take your time. There's an order to this. First you do the open mics, then you do the check spot, then maybe you can be the MC, then you go from five minutes to ten minutes, you start doing other clubs, you have to do some spots on TV, and then you can start closing the show or traveling."

He's staring at his drink. We're in a comedy club uptown. Photos of Jim Gaffigan, Tiffany Haddish, and Dave Chappelle surround us.

Vince drives a Con Edison truck during the day and fixes underground electric lines. He's two years from retirement. He's been doing stand-up comedy for twenty years. He's funny. He's a big guy. I think he's half Hispanic, half African American. He's half something and half another thing. He wears rings on each finger and a big fur coat.

He has this joke I love. He sits on the stool onstage and he relaxes and leans back and he's just having a conversation with the audience.

He says, "I've been stabbed twice. I told this girl I was dating about my stab wounds. She says, 'Ohhh, I like that. You sound dangerous.' I said to her, 'I don't think you understand what stab wounds are. It's the guy that's done the stabbing who's dangerous.'" People always laugh. I laugh.

"When you've been doing it a few years," Vince tells me, "you learn to be in the pocket. Where you got the laugh and you now can take it where you want. You can control the stage. But you have to wait your turn, man. You're just a baby at this. You can't jump ahead. It will happen."

Jon, the manager that night, calls out to me: "James, you're up."

And now I'm all nervous. I've just been told I *can't* skip the line.

I'm about to do forty-five minutes in front of a hundred fifty people. It's my first time doing that long. Vince's been doing it twenty years.

But after what he said, I've lost confidence. Maybe he's right. But it's too late to be scared.

I go through the crowd. Open the door. The MC says, "Here he is, Jaaammes Altucher!"

I'm up.

⬇ ⬇ ⬇

I change careers a lot.

In 1987, while still in college, I start my first business: a debit card for college kids. Debit cards don't yet exist. And companies like Visa and Mastercard are not giving credit cards to college students.

I convince eighty different stores and restaurants to accept the "CollegeCard" and give discounts to all of our members. I program the point-of-sale machines to accept our cards and install them in the restaurants.

I want more equity. I'm doing all the work. A friend tells me, "You're too young. Wait your turn."

I run the entire business for over a year. My two partners in the business graduate. One goes to business school. The other starts working at . . . Mastercard! I'm left alone. I run the business for another six months and then shut it down. It was going nowhere. But it changed my life.

For the first time, I program a computer. And I'm obsessed. I want to switch my major to computer science. I go to the guidance counselor.

She says, "You can't do that. You're going to be a senior. How are you going to take all the classes you need?"

She says, "You have to take four years of calculus; you don't even have one."

She says, "Maybe take some classes in computers, but stick to what you were majoring in. You can't really make a big change like this right now."

But then I do become a programmer. And then I decide I want to write novels. Then I work at HBO. Then I make a TV pilot for HBO. Then I start a company making websites.

Then I sell it and I start a company making mobile software.

I have to raise money for that company. In one meeting someone insists on knowing how it all works.

I say, "Well, first the signal goes up to a satellite and then it beams down to your phone."

"I thought the signal goes to cell towers."

I have no clue. I don't know what I'm talking about. "Well," I say, "sometimes it does that and sometimes it goes into space." That business doesn't work out.

Later, I start a venture capital firm. Then I day-trade. Then I'm a writer. First for one website, then two, then two newspapers, then I write books. Then I write twenty books. Then I start a business selling newsletters and online courses I create.

Then I start a hedge fund and then another one. Bernie Madoff rejects investing in me. I start a business: a social network for people interested in finance. I sell it. I start another business that crowdsources advertisements.

It doesn't work out. So I start something new. And then again. And then I start something again. And again . . . podcasting, writing, investing, several businesses, stand-up comedy.

Throughout this time, I go broke repeatedly. I'm switching careers, but I don't know the three rules of money: making it, keeping it, growing it. I keep losing it. Sometimes people say to me, "You're that guy who keeps going broke," and then everyone laughs a bit.

People often subscribe to a theory that failure leads to future success. This is the furthest from the truth. Does pain lead to creativity? Does failure lead to understanding? Often it does. But it's not a requirement. People show the example that a baby learns not to touch the stove when they first touch it and burn their hand. But I'd rather not burn my hand at all.

It's painful and scary to fail. When you have a family to raise, when you pin hopes on an outcome, when you switch careers in life or switch interests and there's nothing but uncertainty in front of you, these are the times to not dwell on failure but to rely on skip-the-line techniques. How can you turn the energy the world has thrown at you into a force that can catapult you to the top? One answer is the 10,000 Experiments Rule I describe in this book, but it's also important to not indulge in "failure porn." One time I was going broke and there was nothing I could do about it. I was crying and I was outside and it started to rain. I didn't have any energy to get up and get out of the rain. "How could this happen to me, *again!*" I kept thinking, "What misery!" I was scared all the time. Even writing this now, I feel my stomach tighten up. Memory is a form of time travel. It puts your mind and body back into that moment. It's not good and it's not productive. Worrying and anxiety are a waste of energy. Anger is a waste of energy. Do not rent your very valuable mental real estate to emotions or to the agendas of others. Others' agendas will later on turn into your excuses.

But how do you support your family when the world is falling apart? How do you get unstuck when you are stuck to the floor and you have no idea what to do? How do you go upside right when the world goes upside down? How do you learn to start skipping when you always fall?

◆ ◆ ◆

I'm on the stage. I've only been doing stand-up comedy for a few months. I'm scared. I tell a story that is a bit disgusting, a bit nauseating. I think it's funny, but everyone is just staring at me.

The red light in the back blinks on and off, signaling I have to wind it up and get off the stage.

Some guy in the audience yells at me, "Your time is up! Go!" The other people in the audience clap and laugh at what the guy said. I get off the stage.

As I'm walking out, I hear the MC say to the heckler, "Are you OK, sir? Can I get you a free drink?"

The guy says, "I'm here with my two sons. We don't want to hear that shit. That guy was weird."

The MC says, "I'm very sorry, sir."

I leave the club. I go home and I go to bed and feel for a few minutes that I never want to get up again.

But then I *can*. And I *do*.

I want to skip the line, I want to be better, I want to be good at the things I love. I want to change careers. I want to be respected by the people I respect.

I don't want to do the 10,000 Hours Rule. You know the one? It was popularized by Malcolm Gladwell but developed by Anders Ericsson.

The rule is this: if you want to be the best in the world at something, it takes 10,000 hours of what Ericsson calls "deliberate practice."

Deliberate practice entails repetition of a skill you want to get better at, measuring your success or failure, and a coach giving you feedback. Then repeat.

When Michael Jordan was cut from the varsity team in high school because he wasn't yet good enough, he'd practice shooting baskets all day long. If he missed, he'd figure out what went wrong, adjust his stance, and try again. When he was a top professional, the best in the NBA, he still arrived for practice before everyone else and left after everyone else. He put in his 10,000 hours.

Warren Buffett started investing at an early age. He studied under the famous value investor Ben Graham. Buffett would read all day—annual reports from the thousands of different companies he could invest in. He could measure his success by seeing if an investment worked or not. And he had an excellent mentor who could provide him feedback. By the early 1960s, he'd probably already put in his 10,000 hours, and he became the greatest investor of all time.

In the early 1990s, I participated in some of the first experiments that were being used to test out the validity of the 10,000-Hour Rule. A psychologist named Fernand Gobet was studying all kinds of chess players—chess players who had no experience, chess players who were at the master level and had maybe put in a few thousand hours (me), and chess players who were grandmasters.

Gobet would show five positions for just a few seconds and had us re-create the positions. As expected, the grandmasters could re-create them almost perfectly. People at my level could re-create about half the positions. And amateurs couldn't do anything.

But the interesting part was when he gave all three groups completely random positions—positions that didn't come from a game but where the pieces were put on the board randomly, in defiance of the rules of chess.

All three categories of player performed equally poorly. It wasn't that the stronger players had a better memory. It's just that the strongest players had the best memory for chess—because of the hours of deliberate practice they had put in.

The 10,000-Hour Rule seemed like the only way to get truly great at something.

* * *

It's 2008 and I'm living on Wall Street. In the afternoons I'm appearing on CNBC to provide market analysis.

The markets are all crashing. Articles in the newspapers are calling it "The End of Capitalism!"

I have no job. And once again, despite all my experience at this point, I'm going broke, like most other people.

"Why is this happening to me again?" I thought. "I'm supposed to be smart. But I'm always screwing up. I don't know if I have the energy in me to come back after all these years of struggling and now this. How the hell am I going to get back?"

I had started off with nothing.

I made money from a paper route when I was a kid. I borrowed money for college. I paid it back when I sold my first business.

When I first moved to New York City, I lived with a guy named Elias who gambled on chess in the southwest corner of Washington Square Park. My rent was $300 a month.

We shared one room. He took the couch and I took the futon. I kept my clothes in a garbage bag and would pull out my one suit every morning and walk to HBO.

I was happiest then. After work, I'd go to a pool hall in Astoria and everyone there was from Greece, and they'd shoot pool, play chess, and play the three different kinds of backgammon that were popular in Greece. We'd play all night, then I'd go home, put on my suit, and walk to HBO. I had no money at all. I made $42,000 a year, which meant I was taking home about $2,500 a month. Just enough to pay rent, my student loans, and then to eat occasionally.

But I was happy. I loved working at HBO. I loved playing chess all night. I was young and felt like every possibility was in front of me.

But then everything changed. First, I got "the disease." After I started my first company, made money, then lost it, I couldn't stop regretting that I had lost my kids' future. That's a symptom of the disease. I only wanted to make the money back, and I was miserable for over a decade trying to do it.

And then there was 9/11, and then there was the 2008 financial crisis.

The world changed. Nobody wanted to hire anyone anymore. Everyone I knew was changing careers, but nobody seemed happy.

I wanted to change careers too. I wanted to stop caring about the money so much. I wanted to do what I loved, but only if I could be good at it. I wanted to be the best at something.

In this one short life, is it possible to be so good at something that you feel the pleasure, the sense of accomplishment, the feeling of freedom and joy that comes with mastery? And then make money doing that thing you love?

Can I have that?

CHAPTER 1

YOU *CAN* DO THAT

There's B.C. and A.C.

"Before coronavirus" and "after coronavirus."

When the entire world shut down, everything turned upside down. Tens of millions lost their jobs, lost their careers, and suddenly realized that nobody was loyal to them.

When the economy came back, so many people were left unemployed. So many businesses had just disappeared. The institutions we trusted—college, government, whatever support systems we thought we had—had all either disappeared or changed and let us down.

I have to change. I have to find something I can do that I love. I have to get good at it—good enough to make money, enough money so this won't happen to me again.

These weren't my words but everyone's words.

Society was reinventing itself. And nobody wanted to be left behind.

But how do you find what you love? And how do you get good at it quickly? Is it going to take 10,000 hours?

I don't have 10,000 hours. I have to feed my family now!

For the first time, the entire world is in the same situation. We all have to figure out what we are going to do next. And how will we do it? And how will we succeed at it?

How will we find freedom so that nobody can tell us what to do?

How can we master something so we feel the respect of our peers, so we make money, so we can appreciate the nuances of whatever our passion and purpose are?

How can we relax enough to enjoy time with our friends, our family, our community?

Is it too much to ask?

For the first time in the history of the human species, the entire globe came together to focus on a single purpose—dealing with a pandemic. But just as easily as the world came together, it also fell apart. We were left on our own to figure out what we love, how we can get better, how we can help, how we can be safe, how we can thrive.

But now what?

We have to rebuild an economy that was put on life support, a society that was gripped with fears, and each of us as individuals who needed to learn how to deal with massive amounts of uncertainty. Life wasn't meant for us to live by someone else's playbook. We need to call the plays.

Many of us will have to skip the line.

▼ ▼ ▼

The human brain loathes uncertainty.

When one of our ancient ancestors was walking by a bush and suddenly the leaves on the bush started to rustle, our paleo grandpa would either assume it was just wind rustling through the leaves . . . or a lion waiting to pounce and feast.

The human was uncertain! So cortisol would spike, triggering a flight instinct, and our ancestor would run away from the perceived danger. The paleo people who did not run are not our ancestors for a reason. One in a thousand times, they got eaten . . . until the people who didn't mind uncertainty no longer existed.

We have a fear of uncertainty baked into our genes. The strands of DNA that survived in us, that evolved in us, express that stark naked fear of uncertainty.

A modern example of this is the stock market. Often it doesn't matter if the news is bad or good, the stock market will go up. But if the news is *uncertain*, the market will crash. The stock market is a great barometer of the level of uncertainty in the world. If Apple says, "Our earnings will be down," the stock of Apple may or may not go up or down. But if Apple says, "We don't know what our earnings will be," its stock will certainly crash.

But society has evolved faster than humans. We no longer move around in tribes of thirty where we know everyone in the tribe. We no longer move around in larger groups of 150 where, even if we don't know someone intimately, at least we know someone in the group who does. The invention of gossip was incredibly useful in determining if someone was trustworthy enough to go hunting with.

And we kept evolving to more complex and disparate organizations. We formed villages, then cities, then city-states, then kingdoms, then empires, then religions wrapping a single belief system around billions of people.

Life became complex.

As primates, when we are in a tribe of thirty, we're in a hierarchy, a line from alpha to omega and everything in between. Every chimpanzee knows exactly where they stand in the hierarchy. The alpha male has benefits: sex with all the females, a place to sleep in the center of the tribe to get the most protection, the pick of the food.

But the omega doesn't have it so bad either. The alpha always has to protect his position and fight to maintain it. The omega has less food and has to sleep on the fringes of the group, but he also doesn't have to spend his days and nights fighting to maintain his position.

Humans don't have just one tribe but multiple tribes and multiple hierarchies we can belong to or contend with. Where you stand in the hierarchy—how close you are to the top—determines your pay, your responsibilities, even who your friends are and your potential to attract a spouse. Titles, rankings, and other trappings of success become the all-important measure of your worth and your potential.

Are you the junior system programmer? Or are you a manager, director, VP, senior VP, executive VP, chief operating officer, or chief executive officer?

If you are a tennis player, where are you in the rankings? If you are a golfer, what's your handicap?

If you write books, how many did you sell? Or what awards have you won?

It used to be if you were kicked out of the tribe, you would die. There was no other tribe to go to. You'd have to wander into the jungle and hope for the best, but sooner or later you would be eaten. Obviously the stakes are lower now in the modern world, but our instincts to fit in and stay in line are still intact. When it seems like we are going to lose our status in the tribe, several neurochemicals kick in that cause an enormous amount of stress. Cortisol triggers the fight-or-flight response. And tachykinin is triggered when we experience or fear isolation. Both are related to our safety within the tribe. Less safety means more of those bad neurochemicals and more stress.

Other neurochemicals trigger a greater feeling of happiness, but they are not "happy chemicals" as we normally think about them. It's not just about our internal happiness. These neurochemicals are specifically related to where we rank in the tribe.

Dopamine is triggered when a reward is in sight. When we see food and we are about to get it, dopamine tells our brain that if we get that food, our ranking in the tribe might go higher, so it feels good enough for us to take some risks and climb the tree and get that food.

Serotonin is triggered when we have the food: when we have status in the tribe so that we know we will eat and we feel safe. Despite serotonin being a brain chemical, 90 percent of it is made in the gut. Humans eat better when their rank in the tribe is safe.

And oxytocin is triggered when we feel the bonds of friendship and love in the tribe: when we do service for others, when we feel gratitude, when we love someone who loves us back. Again, this inspires us to be the best person we can be because when oxytocin is triggered, yes we feel happy, but we are also further securing our position in the tribe.

So the urge to get in line is strong and deep.

But now we don't have just one tribe. We have many. There's our work tribe, our family tribe, the various tribes related to our hobbies. Are we in line for a promotion at work? Does our spouse love us? Are we beating our friends at the golf club?

And then when we are kicked out of a tribe (when we lose a job, get divorced, have a bad day of golf at the club, bomb performing stand-up comedy), we feel a sense of panic. An ancient panic.

Uncertainty creeps in . . . which triggers stress.

And staring at computer screens all day with a steady stream of bad news, angry emails, and social media skirmishes coming at us only makes it worse.

We start to have this low, simmering, never-ending trigger of fight-or-flight.

And it gets worse when the world falls apart, as it seems to do with increasing regularity every decade. September 11 was bad. The 2008 financial crisis threatened the economy of the entire planet. And the coronavirus was . . . I don't know—it was either going to kill us all or kill the entire economy and bring us to a state of total Mad Max anarchy.

Living with uncertainty has become critical to success.

During these times of crisis, everyone tunes into the news. They are trying to find some certainty, some piece of information that can help them calm down and say, "Phew. OK, I can see the light at the end of the tunnel."

But sometimes that light's not there. Will this crisis mean my job is lost? My career? My hobbies? My routine?

We may have to switch tribes if we have to change careers or jobs, or move, or leave our families, or suffer a loss. We may have to start at the bottom of a new hierarchy all over again. How long will it take us to climb back up to where we were before? Why can't we just start at the top?

"You can't do that!"

You can't just step into a new tribe and become the alpha!

But maybe you can.

I've been forced to switch jobs, careers, interests, purpose, and skills so many times I've made it a personal mission to get good at getting good as fast as possible.

I didn't want to wait 10,000 hours. But I didn't want to take short-cuts either. There's no way to cheat the system. But there are methods for skipping the line, for achieving what you need to achieve using the techniques that I've painfully had to go through again and again.

Every time there's a crisis, either societal or personal, people start talking about the "new normal."

As if everything that was normal before is now going to completely change. What will that new normal look like? What will happen?

The key to skipping the line is to constantly live in the world of "not knowing." To constantly be curious but not threatened by what's next. To live in the world where everyone else is scared but you are so comfortable with the land of not knowing that you can still navigate the rough waters.

Not only do you navigate these waters, but you become a beacon. It's foggy outside. Many people—some old friends, some new friends—are trying to find their way to shore on this foggy and windy and rainy night. You are the beacon and the lights are on. You help them to shore.

This is not the end of the line. This is the beginning.

CHAPTER 2

THE 1 PERCENT RULE

In 2002, I needed to get better at investing. I had lost everything. I had no career. No job. And when you lose everything, you find out quickly who your friends are. In my case, I had no friends left.

I wanted to be a professional investor. I wanted to invest my own and others' money and build up and have a career. I was starting from scratch. Worse than scratch. I was broke!

I kept regretting everything I had done that got me to that point. And I was feeling anxious that I was destined to be a failure—that the future held nothing good for me. I vaguely remembered points in my life when I had felt happiness, but they seemed so distant and so out of reach for me. And I would look at my two daughters and think that I had ruined their chances of having a good childhood or having a father they could admire and look up to.

I took long walks every day. I'd wake up super early and walk around downtown Manhattan before anyone else was awake. And then at night I would take even longer walks, until I was sure everyone in my house would be asleep. I didn't want to run into anyone I knew, even in my own house.

But at one point I started to get excited about the idea of writing a book. And I also started to get excited about an approach to investing that I had been working on. Every day I worked a little harder. I studied every aspect of the investment business, a business I had no expertise in at all. I read books about the history of investing, I wrote software to model the stock markets, I met with other investors and asked them questions. I was learning and getting better each day.

When you get excited about something, your heart lights on fire. That fire propels you to learn more, to study more, to work a bit harder. And by the end of the day you look back and instead of being filled with regrets that have lasted years, you find yourself satisfied with the events of that single day that is now shutting down.

I would say to myself, "I got a little bit better today," and I knew that laid the foundation for having an even better day the next day. Getting a bit better every day shortened the amount of time I would spend each day on time traveling—traveling into the land of embarrassment and foolishness and regrets from the past or traveling into a future filled with spiderwebs of uncertainty and anxiety.

Within two years, I was running a hedge fund with millions invested, I was writing my first book, I was writing a column for the *Financial Times*, and, a few years after that, I sold an investment-related business for millions.

Then, unfortunately, I went broke again!

But still, I had started to put together the methods that would pull me out of darkness again and again. I never took the time to understand then what was happening. It was only later that I had to ask myself, "Why is this always happening to me?" And instead of just getting good at whatever it was I was passionate about, I would eventually become passionate about simply feeling good with today, knowing it would be the cornerstone, the building block for everything that was to come.

▼ ▼ ▼

A full-time job is 2,000 hours a year. But when you first start a new career or want to get good at a new skill, you don't have 2,000 hours a year. You have to be able to pay the bills, to support a family. And what if after 10,000 hours you become interested in something else? Are you really going to spend ten to twenty years of your life mastering something and then never use that skill?

What if you knew a secret method of training that would catapult you right past all of the professionals in your chosen field?

An example: If you play golf, you can spend 10,000 hours practicing your swing in different situations. You can get good feedback from a coach and keep repeating your swing. Within 10,000 hours you'll be great, maybe among the best in the world.

But about thirty years ago, with the rise of Tiger Woods and a new generation of golf professionals, research by scientists and coaches discovered that one attribute can speed up the process of getting great at golf: leg strength. If you put more emphasis on weight training for your legs and lower body, you will have more power when you are hitting a golf ball. What if a golfer had known that forty years earlier? Let's say he kept the secret to himself and didn't tell anyone. He wouldn't need 10,000 hours to get as good as the top professionals. Who knows how much he would need? Maybe that one piece of knowledge would allow our aspiring pro to quickly skip 2,000 hours. We don't really know.

So I started trying a new approach to getting good at something, and by interviewing hundreds of peak performers in nearly every area of life, I noticed that many of these high-performing artists, businessmen, entrepreneurs, investors, artists, writers, actors, etc. also often used this same approach.

It can be applied to rising to the top of a career, learning a new skill so that you quickly end up in the top 1 percent of your field, or even building your network and relationships so you can take advantage of future opportunities that come your way.

There's no such thing as a "straight line" in careers anymore. Each crisis we face changes the world even more. Jobs are lost. Industries disappear. The nature of work changes. People's interests and passions change.

So, what if you want to make it to that top 1 percent of your field as quickly as possible?

$$\blacktriangledown \quad \blacktriangledown \quad \blacktriangledown$$

In this book, we will do away with the 10,000-Hour Rule—the rule that says if you work at something for 10,000 hours you will be among the best in the world at that thing.

That rule no longer works, if it ever did. I found that in my own life, being able to construct experiments to quickly try out ideas, learn from them, and move on from them beats the 10,000-Hour Rule. I call it the 10,000 Experiments Rule.

It's a way of approaching change and crisis by using a set of tools to help with creativity, execution, persuasion, productivity, and leadership—all of which, when working together, will catapult you higher than you ever thought possible and at a speed that everyone will tell you is impossible.

I'm not saying this because I did a research project. I'm saying it because I *had* to do it. Often because my interests and passions changed or merged. Or, worse, often because I was broke and was forced to find success in a new field, and I had to do it quickly in order to feed my family.

Science is important. But the best laboratory is your life. The best scientist is yourself. The best experiments are when you try to do what has never been tried before. This is the research lab and this is where the discoveries are made—the only place to make discoveries that work for you and that reflect your unique perspective on the world.

Dick Fosbury was a high jumper in the 1960s. He was mediocre at best. The technique for high jumping then, the "upright scissors technique," involved running straight toward the bar while facing it, jumping, and then lifting your legs higher than the bar while you leapt over it.

Fosbury simply couldn't do it. His legs were long, so he'd always clip the bar and never get to the heights everyone else was reaching. He did an experiment one day. He jumped backward. He approached the bar with his back toward it and then leapt with his back still facing the bar—completely the reverse of everyone else.

His high school coach begged him to stop. "It won't work. You can't do this." He wouldn't let Fosbury use it in official competitions, but when he saw Fosbury flip backward (in what is now known as the "Fosbury Flop") in a freshmen competition, he said, "OK, let's try it."

Fosbury went from mediocre in high school to winning the gold medal at the 1968 Olympics just a few short years later. First everyone laughed, then everyone told him not to do it, and then every high jumper switched to his method.

He used his knowledge of the sport to create a unique perspective. He won a gold medal. And he changed the sport forever. He didn't do it by practicing 10,000 hours more than everyone else. He did it not by falling into line but by stepping out of line. He skipped it.

And you can too.

The first technique to master is the 1 Percent Rule. Understanding this principle shows how with a tiny effort every day, you can develop the tools needed to quickly become among the best in the world in any field you want. Here's how it works.

If you have $1 in a savings account and the account pays 1 percent interest *per day*, then in 365 days you will have $37.78.

In other words, your "investment" of $1, compounding at 1 percent per day, would make you almost 3,800 percent within a year.

I sometimes say this to people and they say, "Why wouldn't it be 365 percent?" That would give me just $3.65 at the end of the year.

A big difference from $37.78.

But compounding is like magic.

In one day, your $1 becomes $1.01 (1 percent more than $1).

But on the second day, it's not $1.02, it's $1.0201 (1 percent more than $1.01). And on day three it's not $1.03, it's $1.030301 (1 percent more than $1.0201).

And so on. That's compounding.

It starts off small, but the end result is enormous.

I had a friend, Rob, who loved playing chess. I played with him for twenty years. He was good, but he never studied the game, never attempted to get better. And that's fine. It's good to be satisfied with where you are and be happy with it.

But I could tell Rob wanted to get better. He would be disappointed when he lost, and he would be gleeful when he won. I said to him, "Rob, you have skill. Why don't you take a few lessons or buy a book and study the game a little bit?"

I would tell him the math of the 1 Percent Rule. "If you study just a few chess puzzles a day, you'll get 1 percent better each day, and probably in a year you will be better than almost everyone you know. Your skill, if it can be measured this way, will be 3,800 percent better!"

He would always tell me, "Nahh, I just like playing." And again, that's fine. I wanted him to get better because I could see how frustrated he was when he lost. But everybody makes the choices they want. Perhaps there was some pleasure he got out of being disappointed. I don't know. There's always a reason.

Let's apply it to your career, your passion, your skills, whatever you want to apply it to.

If I want to get 1 percent better every day at cooking, then this means I will be almost 3,800 percent better (or 38 times better than I was) within a year. What does that even mean? It's hard to measure cooking skill, for instance. What does it mean to be 1 percent better at cooking? But it's a way of thinking about things.

If I get a little better each day, I'm not just better than I was when I started, I'm 1 percent better than I was the day before. I'm compounding my skill rather than just adding to it.

It's hard to know what 1 percent of a skill is. But just imagine that you are putting the same determination and focus in each day and there is a way to measure your skill, and now, today, you're going to get 1 percent better than you were the day before.

Cooking is a hard one for me. The last time I cooked anything was years ago on a Valentine's Day. I accidentally left the gas on. Then when I lit a match to relight the gas, the oven blew up. The fire department was called. Flames everywhere. I'm lucky I didn't get burned.

When my girlfriend arrived, she screamed at me: "What did you do!?" She threw the meal I was eventually able to put together onto the floor. That relationship didn't last much longer. But, today, if I wanted to get 1 percent better at cooking, maybe I would learn how to make scrambled eggs. Sounds simple. Then the next day maybe I'd learn how to bake a fish.

That seems like at least 1 percent more skill than the day before.

Maybe then I'd start reading about which sauces to put on the fish. And the next day I'd bake a fish, cut it up, and try different sauces on each part to see which I like the best and compare it with the recipes I was reading. Now I know more recipes and also I've learned about how different flavors mesh with fish. That seems like 1 percent better than the day before. Maybe I would then take lessons. Or maybe I would start applying a technique I call "idea sex"—taking two ideas, letting them mate with each other, and seeing the baby idea that is birthed—which I'll describe in more detail later in the book, and start making Sushi-Ritos. (*Mmmm*, sushi combined with burritos.)

Perhaps one day I want to share my results. I write a blog or a Facebook post about what I am doing. Every week I share a bit more. People start to engage with my posts. I'm the "expert" everyone goes to about Sushi-Ritos. People will share ideas back with me. Or make suggestions. Part of any knowledge learned is when you can tap into the "hive mind." I become 1 percent more known for being that Sushi-Rito guy. And my network expands. Now I'm not only getting better at cooking, I'm also carving out my own little area in the niche.

The Wright brothers collaborated with hundreds of people trying to learn the basics of aviation before that field of science even existed. Collaboration and the sharing of ideas gains knowledge and builds your expertise.

After 365 days, I'll be a lot better than someone who just learns one new fish recipe a day. And using the techniques of idea sex and the 10,000 Experiments Rule, I'll have many opportunities to form a unique perspective on cooking that maybe even world-class chefs won't have.

This doesn't mean I'll be better than a world-class chef. But being "the only" is often more important than being better. Careers are made by the people who bring new ideas to an ancient craft. Many people attempt to be at the top of an ancient craft. But few come up with the Fosbury Flop and add to the entire definition of the craft.

Again, this is a bit subjective. It's hard to say, "I've learned 1 percent more about business today!" That's a hard thing to measure!

At the end of each day, ask yourself, "Did I improve at least 1 percent in my career or skill or whatever I am trying to improve today?" People who do this start off slow but then begin to see amazing results.

> • Coolio wrote rap lyrics every day for seventeen years. In 1995, his hit "Gangsta's Paradise" was the number one song of the year on Billboard.
> • Kurt Vonnegut wrote every day for twenty-five years before he had a major bestseller.
> • Pablo Picasso created two works of art a day. That's more than fifty thousand in a lifetime. It adds up.

"But it's too late for me!" No, it's not. Compounding creates fast results. If you think about skill and even career and networking in terms of compounding, then at any age you can reinvent yourself, apply this philosophy, and be enormously better within just one year.

If I write one thousand words a day, in one day that's nothing. But in one year that's the equivalent of two to three novels. And if my skill improves with each day, perhaps because I'm experimenting with styles, coming up with new ideas for different genres, etc., then I'll very quickly be able to find a niche in writing and have the ability to support it, which will catapult me out front.

This is not being competitive, or trying to "beat" other people at skills they might've spent decades building. It's never about that (although that will happen). It's about being able to do what you love, reaching a level where you can make an impact on the world, and quickly rising to a status where you are recognized for it and even paid for doing what you love.

◆ ◆ ◆

There's something else you should know. You can also lose 1 percent a day.

You can say, "Aww, it's only one day. Don't pressure me!" But if you decrease in knowledge by 1 percent a day, then at the end of the year you'll have only 3 percent of the knowledge that you once had. You will have lost nearly all of your skills. People who remain too satisfied, who go to work and do their routine and don't focus on that 1 percent of improvement and learning, will be outpaced by others and left with excuses like, "Well, that guy doesn't have a family like I do" or "I guess other things were more important to me."

But by using the 1 Percent Rule and other tools in this book—for instance, the 50/1 Rule for increased productivity, or the techniques of "idea calculus" and "frame control"—you will find that you have almost infinite time to make those 1 percent improvements in your life every day.

Everything in this book is interconnected. Skipping the line is not a set of hacks for different situations. Nor is it a set of shortcuts to use when a specific situation arises. It's a way of living your life by allowing your passions to drive your learning, time, and other resources. It's allowing yourself to do what comes naturally to you by getting better at it day by day.

These techniques were not developed in a social psychology re-search laboratory. Yes, many people do this research and write their bestselling books, but often the skills they describe are not practical in real life. The ideas here are built from practical experience, both from my own experiences and from the experiences of many others. You're reading this book because you want to be at the top of your chosen passion, you want to make money doing it, and you want to reach the potential you knew you were meant to achieve. This is your journey and not someone else's that they are trying to impose on you.

Each technique is important. But understanding the 1-percent-a-day improvement is critical to mastering the rest.

It may seem trivial: 1 percent up or 1 percent down. But your decisions about how you spend each day sneak up until they come to define you.

Every day matters.

End of math class.

CHAPTER 3

10,000 EXPERIMENTS

I did an experiment.

I met a friend of mine, J, for breakfast, and he brought his new girlfriend, K. J and K. They told me they just had the "going steady" conversation.

"How'd you guys meet?"

"J-Swipe." Or something like that. I forget. It was an online dating app.

"What does 'going steady' mean when you are both in your forties?" I asked. "I haven't heard that phrase since I was in high school."

J was in his forties. K wasn't. I wondered if "going steady" meant that he gave her a ring or something. There's only so many more "steadies" you have left in you at that age.

They both pulled out their phones. "We deleted all of the dating apps on our phones," K said. But they were both peering at each other's phones before turning their screens to me for confirmation.

Hmmmm! I had an idea! The Going Steady app. It would work like this: Both sides of the couple sign up for the app. Then they select the other person. Then when both sides select each other, the app deletes all the dating apps on their phone. If either one ever downloads a dating app or deselects their partner from Going Steady, the other side gets notified by email. Simple! It could include the following extra features:

> - Notifications on Facebook and Twitter that a couple is "Going Steady"
> - Tracking of anniversaries, gifts, places they go, significant memories, etc.
> - Notifications of major relationship milestones, such as anniversaries, to their friends

Boom!

But what do I do next? Maybe this is a good idea; maybe it isn't. There's no way to know until you start to experiment with the idea.

So what makes a good experiment?

» **IT'S EASY TO SET UP AND DO.** This is critical because you need to be able to run many experiments until you make a great discovery.

» **THERE'S LITTLE DOWNSIDE.** For instance, if you develop a cure for the flu, you don't want to simply take the medication and see if it works. You might die! This is why scientists experiment on mice or in a simulation. Similarly, your experiments need to be low risk.

» **THERE'S HUGE POTENTIAL UPSIDE.** If the experiment works, then perhaps this can lead to a million-dollar business, or a successful book, or a promotion, or meeting the love of your life. Who knows?

» **IT'S NEVER BEEN DONE BEFORE.** At the very least, you will have never done it before—this is why you are experimenting. But some aspect of your experiment will probably imply *nobody* has ever done it before.

» **YOU'RE LEARNING SOMETHING.** No matter what, success or "fail-ure," the experiment will teach you something. By doing the experi-ment, you'll either add to your personal knowledge or you'll add to the overall knowledge of the world in some tiny way.

There are *only* two possible results: you either learn something . . . or the experiment succeeds. There is no failure.

Perhaps the most famous experiment that changed the world was when Galileo stood on top of the Leaning Tower of Pisa and dropped two objects at the same time. One was a heavy object and the other was a light object. For nearly two thousand years, people had believed Aristotle—that if you dropped two objects at the same time, the heavier one will fall faster than the lighter one. Galileo's experiment met all five criteria of a good experiment: it was easy, it was low risk, its potential was huge, it hadn't been done before, and, no matter what, he would learn something.

But, and this will be a constant reminder, you can't *think* your way to success. You have to *do*. And to do something, you need to make sure you have limited downside, and perhaps infinite upside. And at the very least, what we think of as "failure" should be recategorized as "learning."

One way or another, Galileo knew he would learn. In 1590, give or take a year (it is unclear in his biographies), he did the experiment. The result: both objects hit the ground at the exact same moment. This set in motion, literally, the development of Galileo's theories of gravity and free fall and the foundation of modern physics.

Through this one experiment, not only did Galileo overturn two thousand years of thinking, correcting the knowledge of Aristotle—who was considered unimpeachable in his intelligence—but he became known as the father of modern physics and even the creator of the scientific method. The 10,000 Experiments Rule catapulted him to the front of the line.

Some people will read a story like this and say, "Well, that was Galileo! I'm no Galileo." But all he did was climb to the top of a poorly built building and drop a big rock and a smaller rock. That's it.

Anyone can do experiments. Anyone can be a scientist of "why?" An explorer of "how?" Read a story like Galileo's and ask, "Why not me?"

With every experiment you do, at the very least you increase your knowledge. Ideally, you increase your knowledge by 1 percent. Yep, it's the 1 Percent Rule in action.

Thomas Edison, of course, is famous for experimenting with 10,000 different types of wires to create the first light bulb. This story is actually false, but it's the one most repeated in schools. He was trying to invent an improved battery. He tried more than 10,000 different battery cells until he found one that worked.

Each experiment had little downside but enormous upside. Edison was able to create General Electric, one of the biggest companies in history, all because of his experiments. When a colleague asked him how he persisted after 10,000 failures, Edison said, "Failures? I didn't fail. I successfully found 10,000 ways a battery won't work!"

For my Going Steady dating app, I needed to figure out a set of experiments that would test my idea. If the experiments succeeded, I would make *millions*!

The next day I spent about an hour outlining what the app would look like: how people would sign up, how they would "connect" with the person they were going steady with, and how the phones would then delete all the dating apps and perhaps send a notification to each of the couple's social networks.

Then I listed the "spec" of the app that I had just dreamt up on Freelancer.com. Freelancer.com is a site where programmers from around the world can see your spec and then bid to do the project for you. It's known as a reverse auction because, all things being equal, whoever bids the lowest will win.

But my experiment depended on hiring the right programmer. I asked each person who bid—and bids were coming in from India, Malaysia, the United States, and all over the world—one question: "Is it possible for an app on your phone to see what other apps exist on the phone?" Why? Because the Going Steady app would have to see your other dating apps. One programmer responded and said, "On Android, yes. On the iPhone, no."

There, experiment finished. The idea didn't work. I'm not going to pay money and make this app if it only works on Android phones. Why is that? Because I did a little more research (five seconds using Google) and saw that 82 percent of teenagers (my target audience) have iPhones, so this wouldn't work.

My great app idea was already a failure after the first experiment. But did it meet the criteria for a good experiment?

- » **EASY TO SET UP AND DO?** Yes. I had the idea, I specced it out, and I uploaded the spec to Freelancer.com.
- » **LITTLE DOWNSIDE?** Yes. I spent zero money. And it was about an hour of my time.
- » **HUGE POTENTIAL UPSIDE?** Yes. If my little experiment on Freelancer .com worked, then I would have hired my programmers, made an app, and started creating experiments to market the app. If the app worked, there would be a huge potential to perhaps sell it to an acquirer.

» **NEVER BEEN DONE BEFORE?** Yes, I had never done it before, so I learned something. From initial poking around, it appeared that nobody had ever made a Going Steady app. So now maybe I can experiment further to see if this is a decent app. Maybe I can be the first to make it.

» **LEARN SOMETHING?** Yes. I learned how to use Freelancer.com and saw that it was a good place to find programmers for later projects. I learned how to spec out a mobile app. I had never done that before. I also learned something new about programming mobile apps and businesses for iPhone and Android.

Sure, it may have been a dumb idea. Hardly worth the time. And yet . . . the experiment took me an hour and cost me zero dollars. And the story of how I experimented with this app idea has become a case study I use in paid talks I give about the 10,000 Experiments Rule. So in that sense, the experiment has paid off.

What I'm talking about is an entirely different method from the 10,000 hours of practice that you've heard of. It's about figuring out 9,000 ways *not to do* something, which may lead you to one or two ways *to do* something, which may lead you to create one of the most popular apps or largest companies in the world.

It's not practicing something repetitively with a coach.

It's about small ways of stretching your knowledge and perhaps the knowledge of the world.

If you do this every day, improving by 1 percent a day, then your knowledge, your skill, your career will improve exponentially in a very short amount of time.

➥ ➥ ➥

A friend of mine had an idea. She had a technique for making tie-dyed shirts, sweatpants, surgical masks, etc. in a unique way. I don't know . . . *she* thought it would be interesting. That people would want it. And she wanted to put "Made in America" on each item. She showed me the shirts. I thought they were beautiful and would sell . . . but what do I know? She spent a week trying to find where to get the materials she needed in America and how to do the manufacturing in America.

"You don't need to do that," I said. "Do an experiment."

"But I still have to find out how to make it," she said. "And I have to find out how to get the materials so I can use the 'Made in America' tag."

"That's fine. But do this: Get everything you need in China. You already know you can get it all in China. Then put on the 'Made in America' tag."

"But that's lying."

"No, you're not going to sell it. You just need a prototype. Put it on a website like Etsy and see if you get orders. If you get the orders, then you figure it out. People will be fine if it takes time. Just say it's custom-made."

"What if I don't get enough orders?"

"Then send everyone their money back."

She paced around the room. "I like it!"

"But wait, you don't even have to do that," I told her. "Scratch everything I just said. Just make an ad on Facebook selling the product. Use a small budget. Like two hundred dollars."

"But what would they click on? I don't even have a website."

"It doesn't matter. They will click to nothing. But you'll be able to see in the Facebook Ads Manager how many people clicked. If there are clicks, then you know people are interested in the idea. If there are no clicks, you don't have to waste your time."

"I like it!"

Viewing her idea as a hypothesis to test via experiments saved her six months of time. In a single afternoon she could've photoshopped a realistic version of the product, made ads, and then determined if her idea would be successful. If the experiment failed, then it's still a success. She saves six months, she learns Facebook Ads, she learns a little more about the demand people have for different ideas in clothes. She could even experiment with more designs, more colors, other labels besides "Made in America." Just for the heck of it, she could try "Made in the Vatican"! Whatever she wants.

What did she do?

Nothing. She got interested in something else.

No problem. All the more reason to do experiments, because it's so easy to lose interest in something you weren't that passionate about in the beginning.

In these examples, the experiments didn't result in successful businesses. Ninety-nine percent of ideas don't work out. That's why experiments have to be easy to set up and have very little downside.

But time was saved. Knowledge gained. And this is the way to go from success to success. There will be experiments that will work. But there will be many more where knowledge is the holy grail.

In keeping with the 1 Percent Rule, I like to do tiny experiments every single day.

For instance, if you are learning chess, maybe try a rarely played but very tricky opening variation you've never tried before, and because it's rarely played, most players will be unfamiliar with it. Study it for an hour using a computer to help you prepare. Then go to one of the online chess sites and play a few games with that opening. No downside. Big upside if people are so surprised by the opening that they don't know how to respond to the particular tricks of that opening. You'll learn something because you'll then run each game you play through a computer and study what you could've done better. And if it works, you can be the expert in that opening and win many games.

Sometimes when I write, I try to experiment.

Maybe I'll write a blog post in the second person (using "you" instead of "I"). Maybe I'll write a post in the form of letters back and forth between me and my grandchildren (an epistolary blog post).

Novelist Tao Lin tried an interesting experiment: his novel *Richard Yates*, about a love affair between two teenagers, is written heavily in the form of text messages back and forth between the two main characters.

Andy Warhol is known for creating "pop art," the idea of using commercial images or celebrities and then mass-producing those images, blurring the distinction between art and American pop culture and commercialism.

But before that, he spent more than a decade in New York City as one of the best illustrators in the advertising industry. He was known as the most realistic illustrator in the business. In other words, his artistic ability was so good that his work was practically photo-realistic. But that's not what makes an art career. An artist that sells his artwork has to stand out and move the needle on the idea of what "art" even is. Warhol was always experimenting with new ways to make his illustrations stand out. For instance, he would do a drawing with pencil, then use ink or watercolor on top of the pencil, then press another paper against his drawing in order to "print" a mirror image.

Then he started doing sketches and paintings of frames from comic strips. This was an experiment. But he saw his friend Roy Lichtenstein was already doing something similar. Another friend of his gave him an idea: "You've got to paint something that everyone will recognize . . . like a Campbell's soup can."

Perhaps his most famous paintings weren't even his idea. He paid his friend $50 for the idea to paint a soup can. He then experimented further by not just painting one soup can and displaying it but by painting thirty-two soup cans and making the entire display one work of art. That experiment paid off. It launched the entire field of pop art. It propelled Warhol to massive success. Just one of those soup can paintings recently sold for $11.7 million.

The key to successfully experimenting is to be prolific.

Edison had to do 9,000 experiments just to get one invention working. Warhol probably painted or drew thousands of drawings before settling on his unique style. The Andy Warhol Museum in Pittsburgh has seven floors filled with paintings, photos, films, drawings, etc. And that's only a small portion of his work. Picasso painted more than 50,000 paintings in his lifetime. Richard Branson has started more than 300 companies.

The Beatles made twelve albums, each one an entire evolution in style over the prior album. Each record was an experiment. They didn't just get better at their instruments or songwriting; they learned how to experiment and go from the skiff/pop style of their early albums to the complex *Sgt. Pepper's* album, where they mixed in everything from vaudeville music to Indian classical music to rock. Experimenting became the norm for each new Beatles' release.

Experiments help you skip the line.

I did an experiment to start my hedge fund.

I wanted to raise money. I wanted people to give me money that I would invest and I would get a small percentage of the profits. I visited one person and said I wanted to raise money and he laughed in my face. "You lost all your money!" he said. "Why should I give you money?" Another person said to me, "Why did you even ask for this meeting? You didn't brush your hair. You don't have a business card. You don't even work out of an office. I'm not giving you money."

And they were right. I didn't really stand for anything unique. I didn't have a solid vision for how I was going to invest.

I wrote some software. I took every piece of data about every stock in existence since 1945. I modeled it out and used the software to find patterns. For instance, if a company has a bad news event and goes down 20 percent and then is down the next three days, how likely is it to go up on the fourth day? I found hundreds of patterns where the odds were very high it would go up. I would not recommend this approach anymore to anyone, but at the time (2002 to 2005) it worked very well, until many other software people started experimenting with similar ideas.

The experiment was this: I invested my own money. I didn't have a lot. And what I did have, I only used a small percentage of. But the results were good. I was up every month in 2002, which was a horrible year for the market.

At the same time, I was doing other experiments, looking into other ways to make money. But this experiment was working. Eventually I raised money. Even top professional investors were investing in my strategy. It worked.

From a simple experiment that cost me little money and little time, and while I was pursuing several other career opportunities, and with almost no money in the bank, and on the precipice of losing my house,

I started a new business and a new career. I was a professional investor and stayed that way for many years.

◢ ◢ ◢

When someone says, "You can't do that!" they are trying to be important. So important that they think they can tell you what to do with your life.

You look at the person and it's your choice right then: Is that person a mirror? If he is a mirror, then you might end up saying, almost by reflex, "I can't do that!" And you will believe it.

I look at a mirror and I see me, and I say to myself, "That is what I look like" (and then I might vomit). When you make something else or someone else important, you create a new mirror. You only know who you are when you look toward others to determine your value. The opinions of peers, bosses, family, the media, the government, or a partner start to matter more than your own opinions. And then you lose the connection between your mind and your heart. You've outsourced these items to others. The more you give that power to others, the lower you fall on the hierarchy and the more your behavior will become a feeble attempt to mimic the behavior, ideas, and boundaries of others.

When we were kids, we always stretched the boundaries. If our parents said, "Don't ever go there!" then of course we went there. We played. We experimented. We were curious.

Make sure your motivations and your interests are more than just a simple reflection of the people around you. Skipping the line means that first you have to step *out* of the line. Everyone will look at you funny then because . . . you're *supposed* to stay in the line. "Line up, children!" the teacher shouts. They will be disappointed. They will question your decisions and wonder aloud about your judgment.

They will try to break that connection between your heart and your mind, the only connection that really matters. Your heart is the compass: go in this direction, now turn here, now pivot there, and now here is where all of your dreams and passions and purpose have been waiting.

Then your heart tells that to your mind. And, free of others' mirrors, you become your own source of light instead of simply reflecting the light of others. Your mind begins to use the techniques outlined in this book to create your own unique perspective on the things you love. To create the skills you need to master what you love. To create the ideas and the execution so you can jump to the front, so you can experiment, so you can play, so you can make money, so you can reach that top 1 percent in whatever it is that powers your internal light.

Why do we give others such importance? Why do we let the people around us, even the people we love, dictate who we are, who we should be?

It's because of loneliness. Nobody wants to be alone. "They like me. They really really like me!" We crave that love from others. All I have to do is to not go around this person, to not skip the line, and I will continue to be accepted. Or else, I lose it all.

I get it. I'm afraid all the time. I have to remind myself constantly that in this one short, tiny blip of life we all get to share together, the choice is mine: Is it my life or just a reflection of everyone else's values?

When I was on the way to the CEO of HBO's office, I was told, "You can't do that!" And my colleague was right. I couldn't do that. In the hall of mirrors that I was walking through, I would get lost. I would risk falling and hurting myself. I would risk being alone.

I went to his office. He looked up from his desk and said, "Who are you?"

I pitched him an idea. "HBO has original TV shows. The best

original TV shows. How about we make original shows in this brand-new medium, the web?" I pitched him an idea I had called *III:am* (read as "3AM").

I would go out on a Tuesday and interview people at three in the morning. Why Tuesday? Because if you are outside at three in the morning on a Tuesday night, chances are something is happening and it's probably not good.

He waved his hand and just looked down at the papers on his desk. "Whatever. Sounds good. Just do it."

And I did. For the next two years, I interviewed thousands of people at three in the morning in New York City. I interviewed prostitutes, pimps, drug dealers, and homeless people. I went to Rikers Island, the jail, at three in the morning, and spent time with the people getting bailed out in the middle of the night. I turned over every rock in the city. This became perhaps the first "web show." I posted the interviews on HBO's website for almost three years. The *III:am* web show I was doing was mentioned in *Time* magazine and became one of the most popular parts of HBO's website at the time. I learned how to interview during this period.

HBO gave me money to shoot it as a pilot. They paired me with a well-known documentary producer and for the next year I learned everything I could about making a TV show.

Other companies noticed what I was doing. They would call me and say, "Can you make a website like that for us?"

This allowed me to build up my first company. I was building the websites for almost every entertainment and media company on the planet. I ended up selling that business for millions.

Hearing "You can't do that!" and walking past it broke the mirror. Shattered it. When you are no longer just a reflection is when you start to make a real footprint in the world. It's when you start to gain knowledge.

Reflections have to stay close to the mirror or they disappear. Saying "I can do this" and not being too tied to the result is freedom.

Why do I say "not being too tied to the result"? Because if I know the result, then it's only ego doing the experiment, not a true quest for knowledge.

Not only should nobody be so important as to say "You can't do that!" but no result, no outcome should be important.

It is only in this way that a person leaves the world of mirrors, reflections, ghosts, and ego and enters the world that has been waiting for them this entire time.

I did another experiment.

It was early 2009. After selling three different businesses and making a good living as a writer, I was broke.

There are three skills to money:

- Making it
- Keeping it
- Growing it

I seemed to be pretty good at making it. But I didn't have the other skills. Yet.

I had another idea for a dating website. I had thought about investing in one in 1999 and I had studied the industry. They were the most addictive sites, and now dating apps were the most addictive apps.

Facebook, after all, started as a way for college kids to rate each other.

So I figured, what if I made a dating site that worked with Twitter? You'd sign up for my site (I called it 140Love.com) and the algorithm would look at your Twitter feed and followers and match you with other people based on similarities in your Twitter feeds. Then, before you made your choice, you could see the Twitter feeds of everyone you matched with. So you could really determine which was the right person for you, as opposed to every other dating site.

I wrote the software (and if you don't write software, which I don't anymore, it would cost about $1,500 to make a basic site like this) and then released it. It was doing OK. But not great. Why wasn't it taking off like I hoped? I figured that people would love knowing more about their potential mates before they reached out and made contact. Well, I was wrong. People like dating sites that are mostly anonymous.

Was this a failure? Not at all. It took me about a week to program. And all that time I was busy with other things. I had a daily column in the *Wall Street Journal*. I had a column in the *Financial Times*. I was a regular on various news shows. I was writing a book. But in that week it took me to program, I learned how to use software that could make use of Twitter's API (an interface by which other programs can talk to Twitter to get profiles, tweets, etc.). I learned more about dating sites and how they go viral. I learned the history of the dating industry (always learn the history of whatever field you are excited about). I learned the specific nuances that forced me to close down the site.

And something else totally unexpected happened.

I got a call from one of the top three ad agencies. They wanted to meet. They liked the site and they needed someone who was an "expert" on Twitter. I wasn't an expert, but the fact that I did this site sort of made me seem like one.

They wanted to know if I did "Twitter consulting." I said, "Yes!" They had a client, a major car company, that was releasing a new mostly electric car, and they wanted to get the younger generation involved. They wanted a Twitter strategy.

I started spitting out ideas and they liked them (see chapter 10: "Learn Idea Calculus"). I was hired! Only thing: I'd have to go back and forth to Detroit to spend time with the client. And, oh, by the way, they had many more clients for me.

I knew the agency business well. I ran a web agency in the 1990s, and I knew that if I did a good job and built a real agency, I would eventually sell it to a big ad agency, maybe even the one that was asking me to handle their car client.

But I wasn't sure. Again, so far I had spent little time and little money on this entire idea (140Love.com) and I was at the door of having a real business, one I could build and sell. But I didn't feel in my gut like I was interested.

I'm not a very good networker. I'm shy about calling people. I'm bad at returning calls. And I lose touch with people very easily.

But (and we'll cover the idea of "six-minute networking" in chapter 13: "Microskills Everyone Should Learn") I made up for it in good looks.

(Kidding—wait for the section on six-minute networking.)

I called Michael Lazerow, the CEO of Buddy Media, which was a Facebook ad agency. Brands like Pepsi would come to Buddy Media and get them to set up their Facebook pages, Facebook contests, strategies, advertising, etc.

I said to Mike, "I'm thinking of doing a Twitter version of what you are doing for Facebook."

He said, "Sounds good! Maybe we would even buy you if it really takes off." I heard a lot of noise in the background.

"Where are you?" I asked.

"St. Louis airport. About to go to Tokyo. Then twenty-four hours later going to L.A. Then back here."

What the—

I didn't want to do that. I didn't want to travel all over the place selling selling selling to people I didn't necessarily want to be around.

I had gotten trapped in front of a mirror! First the ad agency: "We think you're great! Go to Detroit!" Then Mike: "This might be great! Maybe we will even buy you!" They like me. They really, really like me. But I had to pull away from the beautiful images I was seeing. There's no mirror for the heart. You have to listen amid the distraction of the tribe, of society, of the people you admire. I simply didn't want to do this business. I don't know why. But, as they say, my heart was not in it.

I said no thanks about going to Detroit. I shut down the business. I moved on. End of experiment. But I learned a lot, and it could have turned into any opportunity I wanted it to be.

That experience helped me for years. Because this was early on in Twitter's life, I used my in-depth knowledge to start building an audience. I experimented with doing a Q and A session on Twitter. I had never seen anyone do that before. For two hours I answered questions about entrepreneurship and investing, and then people started asking random questions about anything and I started answering those. I loved it! And more people started following me on Twitter. I was building an audience. An experiment that cost me zero dollars and two hours of time was a success. I did it a week later, and then a week later. I did these Q and A sessions every Thursday for six straight years.

Sometimes people would ask me, "Who are you? Why should we ask you questions?" They were trying to establish status over me. What were my credentials? I would answer honestly. "I'm nobody." As long as people were still asking questions, I would simply answer.

There were many results to this experiment. One is that it helped me when I was selling books. Eventually I visited Twitter's offices and became friends with Twitter's then-CEO, who ended up writing the foreword to my book *Choose Yourself!*

That one experiment changed my life even though it can be viewed as a total failure. When you learn, you earn. And every experiment you learn from will allow you to skip the line.

Because of the knowledge from that experiment (among many other experiments), I was able to use my platform on Twitter to self-publish a book at a time when very few people were doing it. It reached the number one spot in the entire Amazon store—perhaps one of the first self-published books to ever do that. That helped me build a relationship with Amazon.

I skipped the line in bookselling and went from zero to hero. My prior books had never made it to the bestseller list, but the first major self-published book I wrote did—and almost all of my marketing was done via Twitter.

Again:

- Easy to set up and do
- Little downside
- Huge potential upside—maybe multiple opportunities for upside
- Unique—never been done before as far as I know
- Learned something—I learned, and I didn't go to Detroit.

And instead of spending 10,000 hours learning how to self-publish and market a book (or even start an ad agency business focused on Twitter), I was able to go to the front of the line.

All because of a little experiment.

I'm always attempting various large and small experiments. Some of them seem quite stupid to the people around me. But they know me now, so they laugh and hope for the best. Other experiments are, again, designed to teach me something new with very little downside but huge upside. I never think about the outcomes. When my curiosity is active, I know that my heart is talking to my mind and that something is worth pursuing.

Right now I will tell you a few of the experiments I am trying where I both learn and, perhaps, accomplish.

Because I spent many years as a programmer and many years as a podcaster, I'm interested in the surge of users of videoconferencing software. Zoom, for instance, added something like 200 million daily users during the lockdown.

But as a podcaster, Zoom is very lacking. And none of its competitors are any better.

I pulled out my waiter's pad (more on this later) and started writing down my "ten ideas of the day" (see chapter 9: "Exercise the Possibility Muscle"). I came up with ten features I'd like to see added to Zoom. I did initial research on how I would engineer it from a software perspective and then the next day I did a list of "Ten Programmers I Should Talk to About This."

I decided to do an experiment. I wanted to implement the software this time rather than just send another company the ideas.

I found a programmer, we spoke, and I liked him very much. We agreed to work together and I kept throwing more and more features at him while he started developing the software. Minimum downside for both of us, and if the software solves many of the needs of podcasters and even event organizers, then it could be a huge business. At the very least, I'm learning many of the nuances of doing remote podcasts, an area that is important to me and will increase the quality of my podcasts.

Conducting 10,000 experiments, or even far fewer, can lead to great knowledge and great success, and it's the quickest way to skip the line to the top of any profession with as little downside as possible. As Jigoro Kano would say, "Maximum efficiency, minimum energy."

CHAPTER 4

BECOME THE SCIENTIST OF YOUR OWN LIFE

Tracy Morgan stopped by Stand Up NY, the club I am part owner of. In case you didn't know it, he's one of the most famous stand-up comedians in the world and was one of the stars of the hit TV show *30 Rock.*

The manager said to him, "Want to go on up?"

He said, "I got nothing. I got nothing . . . Ahh, whatever. I'll go up. I'M TRACY MORGAN!"

He went up for twenty minutes just spewing jokes nonstop. Everyone was laughing.

He had this raw energy. He was shouting and laughing. And making faces. It was like there was no filter between his brain and the audience. He pointed to all the people sitting up front. "Your parents had sex and your parents had sex and your parents had sex . . . We're all here because your dad put his . . ." And so on. Just the way he said it. *Boom!*

He said to me at the bar afterward, "Just say what's on your mind. You got troubles? Talk about it. That's what they want to hear."

This was the scary part for me: I was given the choice by the manager of the club to perform *before* Tracy Morgan or *after*.

I've been given this sort of choice many times. And I've seen others given this choice. Everyone immediately says, "Before."

How come? Because a comedian like Tracy Morgan (or any top comedian) is going to "lock up" the audience. They will be so charmed by his energy, his fame, his raw uniqueness that the comic performing afterward will always feel like a letdown to the audience.

"I just saw Tracy Morgan!" is what they will be thinking if I go onstage. Or, "I just watched Jim Gaffigan!" or "Tiffany Haddish!" It doesn't matter who. But what's for sure is this: after seeing a famous and skilled superstar, the crowd will be disappointed by anyone who follows after.

I said, "After." This was going to be my experiment of the day. You only get better if you lean in to the uncomfortable. The room least crowded is the room you learn in.

Tracy was walking down the steps from the stage and he shook my hand. I took the microphone from him. People started to get quiet.

I could have chosen "before." This would be the 10,000-hour way. Repeat my material. Look at the videotape afterward (I always video-tape my sets), learn from what I observe on the video. Then repeat. And repeat and repeat until I crossed that magical threshold of 10,000 hours.

"Before" is the comfort zone. The comfort zone, of course, is comfortable. Who would choose to leave it? But the path to mastery is in the room least crowded. "Be the *only*." You don't get many opportunities to get out of the comfort zone. Nor would you want to. Who wants to be uncomfortable all the time?

An experiment is always outside the comfort zone. You become an explorer of the places nobody else wants to go.

"Before" is the 10,000-Hour Rule. But I don't have 10,000 hours. "After" is the 10,000 Experiments Rule. It's in the discomfort zone, and the experiment you do might explode.

⬇ ⬇ ⬇

You know something is a valid experiment when you take what you normally do, get curious about an idea, as in "What if I try . . . ," and then, you suddenly feel fear. You suddenly feel as if someone is yelling, "You can't do that!" or "You shouldn't do that!" Or you feel "What if people don't like me after this?" That fear is what's most important.

Then you are the only person on the other side of *can't*. That is success.

Each experiment lets you skip part of the 10,000 hours. Because everyone else can't do what you just did.

I know this because I've done it. You can fail on 10,000 experiments but then suddenly you're Thomas Edison.

That's why people who put in years of invisible work often seem like overnight successes.

I used to cry after failing. Sometimes I still do. It's so painful. I always feel like giving up. That's why I've learned to keep the experiments small.

Tomorrow is always another day. A new experiment.

Perform 10,000 experiments and you can't help but become the best in the world. (Actually, I suspect about a thousand would be good enough, but why stop there?)

⬇ ⬇ ⬇

With stand-up comedy there are many ways to experiment:

1. Perform after someone really good, as I did with Tracy Morgan. The audience starts off not liking you. Win them over.

2. Do the "check spot"—the spot when the drink and food checks are being handed out by the waiter and everyone in the audience is talking. You get really good at learning how to entertain a drunk audience that is trying to figure out what 15 percent of $22.58 is so they can leave a tip.

3. Host. It gives you a chance to do six mini-sets. You get really good at reading the energy of a room and bringing it back up.

4. Go up first. Because the crowd is not fully warmed up yet. Children laugh three hundred times a day; adults laugh only five times a day. If they are not warmed up, they still don't remember how to laugh.

5. Go up last. Because the crowd is tired and drunk.

6. Do 100 percent crowd work. Crowd work is when you just talk to the audience instead of using material you've prepared in advance. You have to be really sharp and in the moment. "You're from Buffalo and you install floors?" And then you have to make a joke out of that. A hundred times in a row. ("What's there before the floor? Is it just a hole into space? If you're already in Buffalo, you've probably hit bottom. People are going to need those floors, so thank you for your service.")

7. Do 20 percent new material every set. Most comedians never do new material and do the same jokes for years.

8. Act out the joke. Voices are funny.

9. Make jokes that will make them hate you. Practice dealing with either silence or heckling. Silence is the cruel beast of stand-up comedy.

10. Tell a true five-minute story about your life. It forces you to find, in real time, the funny in your story.

This is proof that *doing* is better than *thinking*. You can only work out your jokes with a hundred strange eyes staring at you and doubting you.

I never know what I'm going to learn in advance. I am the student. I am just doing experiments. Each experiment changes me. I get home and write down what I learned. I skip more hours.

One time I wanted to do an experiment that would help me improve my one-liners. I went on the subway with a friend who could videotape me so I could later watch the video to learn which lines worked the best. Trust me, nobody on a subway wants to see me doing stand-up. This is the toughest crowd. This was an experiment in trying to improve my delivery and my writing so I could always get at least one person to laugh, no matter the situation. I would have to trim the fat on each joke—not even an extra word.

🔻 🔻 🔻

I did OK that night I went up onstage after Tracy Morgan. There's nothing spectacular to report. I didn't wow anyone, but people laughed and it was OK. Same with the subway car. Some people laughed. Most people ignored me. I remember one joke: "I ordered an UberPool, but they sent me this subway car instead." Oh wait, another one: "Is this the 6½ train? Is this subway going to Hogwarts?"

But . . . I learned and I improved. I was afraid in both situations, but I got over my fear and did it. I learned a little bit more about how to deal with a complex and even terrifying problem—another 1 percent improvement. Each experiment gave me more skills and helped me deal with more difficult situations.

I don't even perform unless it gives me a chance to figure out at least one experiment to do. Like one time I played the air piano instead of telling jokes. (I simulated playing "Great Balls of Fire" without a piano in front of me.) That experiment bombed. But I learned. And it took me about a week of practice to get all the hand motions right.

Another time I experimented with giving the audience a choice of what topic I would make jokes about. I never saw a comedian do that before, but I had used that idea in my public speaking (see chapter 5: "Borrow Hours"). When the audience feels like they have a choice, they have a cognitive bias to be more engaged with what you are doing.

That experiment worked.

Every night I experimented. A year later I was performing for forty-five minutes at Carolines, the biggest club in New York City. Six months after that I was asked to tour all over the Netherlands at the biggest clubs. Each club sold out.

I had skipped the line by about ten years. But I am still a student. Still experimenting. Experiments never stop.

CHAPTER 5

BORROW HOURS

She didn't even know the rules!

Maria Konnikova has a PhD in psychology and she's also been obsessed with Sherlock Holmes ever since she was a kid. She wrote a bestselling book: *Mastermind: How to Think Like Sherlock Holmes*.

Then she decided to learn poker and write a book about it. She didn't know the rules of poker. She was a complete beginner.

She worked with a coach, one of the best poker players in the world, Erik Seidel, learned the rules, and started getting strong enough to play in tournaments.

Within a year, she had successfully skipped the line. She had already won up to $250,000 playing in poker tournaments against some of the top players in the world. Some of those players had been professionals for more than twenty years!

I asked her, "Do you feel like you borrowed from the thousands of hours you put into psychology on the way to getting a PhD?"

"Absolutely!"

Her experiences in studying psychology and her obsessive interest in how Sherlock Holmes solves problems gave her an extra edge in poker that most people don't start with. She was better able to read people to determine who was bluffing and who wasn't, and she was better able to make quick decisions, Sherlock Holmes–style. The process of research-ing and studying for her PhD also gave her the discipline to quickly study what she needed to learn and gave her a master-level knowledge of statistics, which is critical for poker.

Erik Seidel, her coach and one of the biggest cash winners in poker history, is also familiar with the concept of borrowing hours. Before playing poker, he was the world backgammon champion.

Some of the skills in backgammon overlap with skills in poker: read-ing your opponent, money management (since backgammon is a gam-bling game), statistics, competitive psychology, having a poker face so nobody can read what you think of the game situations, etc. Note that these skills are not related to each other. Having a good poker face is a completely unrelated skill to money management, and yet both are critical to be a top 1 percent backgammon player or a top 1 percent poker player.

You can borrow hours by applying skills you learned in one field to another. This is a huge advantage. But without knowing that the skills needed overlap with ones you already have, it will take you a long time to make the direct translation.

How did Pelé, perhaps the greatest soccer player ever, get so good so fast? He didn't start playing seriously until he was fifteen years old, an age by which many professionals would have already had a decade of experience and 10,000 hours under their belts.

He grew up in an impoverished family and didn't have access to the facilities or equipment that he and his friends would need to play soccer. Instead, he played another sport popular in Brazil called *futsal*. Smaller balls and a condensed field of play force players to do a lot more footwork and passing. "Futsal makes you think fast and play fast," Pelé said. "It makes everything easier when you later switch to football."

In addition, Pelé would often play barefoot on the hard street, making the later transition to a grass field (with actual sneakers) much smoother. His hours playing futsal as a child easily translated into hours practiced when he switched to soccer, and he almost instantly became the best in the world. He'd borrowed hours from one sport to apply to another.

Whether you are a scientist or a curious individual allowing your passions to lead you in new directions, you don't know the outcome your efforts will produce. You might have a guess about the outcome, but no matter what, you have to let the result wash over you and change you. Being detached from the results is not only the most important rule of science but the most important rule for skipping the line.

Not to mention relationships too.

I've often been insecure in my relationships. I try too hard to please. When I do this, it's not because I am a giving and kind person. It's the opposite. I want to receive, so I am trying to smudge the results of the experiment that began when I first approached the person who I was falling for.

Being detached from the results doesn't mean being heartless, it doesn't mean you don't care, and it doesn't mean you refuse to give of yourself.

In fact, more than ever, you are experimenting, because you are looking for knowledge that can benefit not only those you love but also the world. And in being the source of that knowledge, it will also ultimately benefit you.

If the wants, needs, and prejudices of others, even those you love, take up too much mental real estate in your brain, then you have no room left over to actually be the person you were meant to be—the person who actually has the potential to help others.

The way to become a giving and generous person is to become

detached from the results of experiments, to become detached from the needs of others. You are a visitor from another universe, another dimension, and you are here to unlock the puzzle this universe holds for you, to play with and tweak this puzzle until its secrets unfold.

This is your mission, and it is only solving this puzzle that will truly help the people who you were sent to our world to help. The playful child without fear of the reactions of others is the one who sees the world for what it is: the emperor wears no clothes, the wolf has no bite, and the sky has no limits.

⬇   ⬇   ⬇

Kevin Kelly, former editor of *Wired* magazine, told me, "Don't be the best, be the *only!*"

Finding your own unique perspective is what separates people who have skills from people who will be in the top 1 percent of their field and who will eventually find great success in that field (whether it is monetary success, critical acclaim, or great respect from other masters in the field). When I finally grasped this, after risking it all and losing it all too many times, it became the source of much opportunity and success for me.

In the rest of the book, I'll show you how to identify the microskills you need to develop to skip the line. I'll also show you techniques that will help you put the 10,000 Experiments Rule to work so you can leapfrog everyone else who's plodding along with their 10,000 hours of repetition. I provide examples in a variety of fields, including investing, entrepreneurship, writing, comedy, and more. I will give you a toolbox that you can open when you need to fix something or start something new.

Maybe you'll need to tweak a negotiation. Or learn something a bit faster. Or you'll need to persuade, or be more productive, or communicate better.

You'll need all these things to be the scientist of your life. To conduct the experiments that will allow you to skip the line.

While everyone else is trying to cling to something they can call "normal," you will lean in to the uncertainty that truly defines what life is, and what a successful life is. You'll be able to move forward with curiosity, finding new things to become obsessed about learning.

Curiosity combined with obsession leads to experiments.

Experiments lead to inventions and innovations that are unique, which produces more knowledge, and that knowledge might be unique to you.

Uniqueness plus new knowledge helps you reach the top 1 percent of any field you choose.

And with the world turning upside down after a crisis—doesn't matter which crisis . . . could be a personal crisis, 9/11, a financial crisis, or the Covid-19 pandemic . . . you will experience a life-changing crisis at some point—having the ability to switch interests, even switch careers, and quickly rise to be among the top in the world is going to be invaluable.

You will have new passions and interests throughout your life. You will find new sources of meaning that will excite you the moment you open your eyes. But too often, people say, "I wish I could do that," and then they get ready for work, stick to their routine, and never think about that new passion again.

I get it. It's hard to go against the agendas that society wants for us. It's hard to say "I can" to the people who say "You can't!" But by using the techniques in this book, you will learn to be "the only." You will learn to experiment and reach success in the pursuits you love. You will learn to say "I can," and then to finally say "I did."

CHAPTER 6

BUILD MICROSKILLS

There is no such skill as "business" or "entrepreneurship" or "investing." Or even "software development" or "chess" or "writing."

Any skill worth getting good at is really a collection of microskills. And to get truly great at something, you need to get good at those microskills.

I was the worst entrepreneur.

For one business I started and was CEO of, I'd call my secretary while I was standing right outside the building, 44 Wall Street, and I'd ask her if there was anyone in the hallway. If she said yes, I'd run upstairs, sneak into my office, lock the door, and ignore anyone who knocked on it until I was ready. I was very shy and could barely look people in the eye. Even my mother used to call me "creepy."

I was lucky because I was building websites for Fortune 500 companies during a time when anything related to the internet was booming as a business. So I didn't need that many skills. But to be truly good at business, or entrepreneurship, you need to be good at a basket of microskills. Again, there is no *one* skill called "business."

Here are some of the microskills in business: sales, negotiation, idea creation, execution, leadership, management, marketing, selling the business, project management, follow-ups, networking, delegating (a microskill of management but I'm separating it out). And there are many more.

You don't have to be good at all the skills to run a good business. And being good at one of these skills doesn't mean you are good at any of the others. You have to study and focus on each of the microskills.

In my first successful business, I was good at sales, idea creation, and execution. I was horrible at everything else and had to learn the hard way since I had never even heard of the concept of microskills.

Why was I good at sales?

I had no real sales experience. But in the early days of the commercial World Wide Web, I already had significant experience programming for it. And that gave me street cred. I'd been able to borrow hours from my training as a programmer to apply to my nascent skills as a salesperson. I was excited about the widening consumer usage of the internet, and I was able to convey that excitement when telling companies, for instance American Express, that eventually their entire business would be run via the internet. I was passionate and convincing, and I had enough knowledge to be able to convince others of my vision.

There are many microskills of "sales," but vision and an ability to communicate that vision are high on the list. I was also good at coming up with ideas for my customers. And I was good at developing their websites. So I had three things going for me.

But I really didn't know how to manage employees. I didn't know standard ways of valuing a business. I didn't know, for instance, that a service business (like an ad agency or consulting business) is worth much less than a product business (like a software company).

There's a saying with a service business: "All of your assets walk out the door every night." Whereas there's another saying with a product business: "You make money while you sleep." I didn't know these two sayings, but you can easily guess which type of business is worth more money.

Not knowing this cost me millions of dollars.

The American Express website, for instance, was tens of thousands of pages. So I wrote software that would build all the pages at once using various templates. But I didn't tell them I wrote software because I didn't want them to know that it didn't take me as much time as they thought it would take me.

In other words, I built something similar to WordPress, valued at over $3 billion, in order to complete a service. That service was valued at $250,000. Not saying I built WordPress, but it was a start. A start I should have continued if I had better business skills.

I messed up but had no idea I had messed up. If I spent 10,000 hours doing various business or entrepreneurial activities, it would take me a long time to figure out these basic concepts that I was missing.

In fact, because I quickly sold the business, I thought I was a genius. I thought there was nothing left for me to learn—if I could make it here, I can make it anywhere! I wish I had someone sit me down and tell me, "James, you got lucky! Now you need to learn these ten other skills."

Looking back on that business now, I realize that if I had understood a little more of the basic principles of networking (e.g., that the connections of your connections are a much more reliable source of opportunities than your direct connections), then I would have built a much bigger business. If I had known how to properly manage people, if I had known which aspects of my business were valuable and which were less valuable, I would have had a lot more success with that business. If I was more proficient at "follow up," I would have landed many more customers. I would do the sales pitch, everyone would get excited, but I wouldn't delegate the follow-up properly and would often lose opportunities to my competitors.

Being good at the skill of business requires having some proficiency in, and being aware of, all of the microskills. Business skill is just the basket of all those microskills.

Writing is not just one skill. There are various microskills involved: storytelling (which by itself has many microskills), language play, understanding the different genres, character development, editing, dealing with writer's block, learning how to sell and market your work, etc.

Chess involves knowing openings, middlegames, endgames, open positions, closed positions, tactics, positional play, etc.

Stand-up comedy requires humor (of course), likability, stage presence, crowd work, dealing with hecklers, dealing with silences, voice, storytelling, setup/punchline, act-outs, etc. That's in addition to the social aspects of comedy: dealing with bookers, other comedians, club owners, managers, and the other professional aspects of the business of comedy.

Whatever you are interested in, break out a pad and list at least ten microskills needed for success in that field.

There are the technical skills: for instance, if you want to be an artist, you probably need skills like drawing, perspective, oils, watercolor. Then you probably need to know the history of art so you can figure out how to stand out and be unique. Then there are the "tribal skills"—sometimes called "soft skills"—which can be really hard but are needed to rise up in the art world: networking, communicating about your art, salesmanship.

For each skill you write down, now you need to think of some experiments to start learning those skills.

If you want to learn to program, one experiment is to download whatever tools you need to run a program that just says "Hello" on your computer screen. Now change "Hello" to "Hi there!" That's an experiment.

If you want to learn to cook, here's a fun experiment: Make a menu of crazy dishes that you'd like to eat (once again, I'm going to have to bring up the Sushi-Rito). Invite some friends over and ask them to order off "the menu." Make the food. *Boom!* You're a master chef for the evening.

A friend of mine once wanted to be a professor of computer science. He had a PhD in physics. He applied for a job to be a professor at Cornell University. His girlfriend was living there, which is why he applied there.

They rejected him because he had never been a teacher before and they weren't sure if he knew computer science. "Teaching computer science" may have been a microskill he lacked. So he did an experiment to learn the skill of teaching. He put up a sign at the university: COMPUTER PROGRAMMING CLASSES AT 8:00 P.M. He knew the classrooms would be empty at eight p.m. A few kids showed up the first night. He started teaching them. More showed up the second night. Then more. Then more. He learned the microskills associated with being a good teacher. He built up a following among the students. Preparing for each class taught him more of the skills in computer science he would need to know.

Eventually Cornell hired him to be a professor.

His experiment worked.

❧ ❧ ❧

You master the microskills by borrowing from other skills you might have. For instance, if you know how to speak Spanish, you might have an easier time learning Italian. And then you design experiments that combine the doing with the learning so you quickly move up the ranks of the hierarchy you've defined for yourself.

Back in 1999, I was far from knowing any of this. I had the arrogance of just selling a company and I had lost all sense of purpose, of vision, of the need to constantly experiment, be curious, learn, and increase mastery as a means toward self-fulfillment and well-being.

I had not yet started exercising my possibility muscle (see chapter 9: "Exercise the Possibility Muscle"). Ideas are a muscle just like anything else. If you stay in bed for two weeks, guess what, you might need physical therapy to walk again. You'll need to exercise every day in order to build the leg muscles back up. The idea/possibility muscle is the same way. It must be exercised. If you can't see all the possibilities that are right in front of your face, you will not be able to take advantage of them when the time comes.

But then I started getting excited about investing. I became obsessed with learning everything I could.

You can only be good at the things you are obsessed with. Think about it, all other things being equal, who is going to be better at race car driving? It's the person who is obsessed and studies the history, is excited to try new ideas out while driving on the racetrack, seeks out the best trainers and training techniques, and studies the videos of the best to learn what their unique skills are. You can borrow hours from another domain or you can run a series of experiments to test your aptitude and raise yourself up to the next level.

Once I started thinking in these terms, life became more fun.

Every day I would wonder, "What should my experiment be today?" Some are in development. Some are ongoing. Some just take a few minutes of time. At any given point, I probably have five to ten experiments happening.

But in order for the 10,000 Experiments Rule to bring you to the top 1 percent of your field or higher, you need more.

You need to discover the various passions in life that you want to get better at.

To do this you need to try many things. This is where your heart guides you. You want to try investing? Do it. You want to try to write a book? Start one. You want to try to start a business? Don't ask for permission. Figure out a way to test your idea and start it.

Others' reactions to your experiments are just data. Don't let them be a reflection of who you are. A scientist is detached from the results and uses the data learned from an experiment to guide the next set of experiments.

Always be the fool, the one who innocently doesn't understand.

Be the outsider.

CHAPTER 7

PLUS, MINUS, EQUALS

Brazilian black belt Allan Goes first tried to gouge Frank Shamrock's eyes out. Then Shamrock took Goes's leg, fixed it to his armpit so Goes couldn't move it, and wrapped his own legs around Goes's knee joint, twisting them until Goes's ankle was dislocated. Still, the fight ended in a tie. A few years later, Frank Shamrock was the world champion in the middleweight division of the Ultimate Fighting Championship (UFC).

Being born into a violent family, getting kicked out of that home, and bouncing in and out of the foster care system until finally reaching adulthood—this is often the fastest way to jail and spending most of your life incarcerated. Frank Juarez was heading toward that life.

Bob Shamrock knew this and wanted to help. He and his wife could not have kids, so they started taking kids in through the foster care system. Bob had a unique parenting style: keep them busy, keep them tired, give them something to be proud of, and once they find something they are interested in, double down on it.

He had his foster kids chopping wood, cleaning movie theaters, and doing tons of odd jobs around the local community. He also got each kid a jacket with the Shamrock crest on it. Be proud of who you are and where you come from.

One of the kids, Ken Kilpatrick, was fifteen when he was brought into the Shamrock home, but had already been in and out of the correctional system, had lived in cars, and had no direction in life. Once he moved into Bob's house, Bob saw that Ken loved sports. He suggested Ken try out for the school wrestling team, but only if he kept up at least a C average. Ken quickly became the best in the school at wrestling and started learning boxing and martial arts.

A few years later, another young boy who had been in a dozen foster care homes before reaching Bob joined the Shamrock household. Frank Juarez was also into sports, particularly the style of martial arts that Ken was beginning to teach. Bob was the mentor to both, giving them the discipline and work ethic to stay focused.

Ken taught Frank a style of martial arts called "submission fighting." The idea is to control your opponent and use various techniques to get them to submit, or "tap out," in a fight. Ken started a training facility, the Lion's Den, and Frank became one of the first fighters he trained.

Both men changed their last name to Shamrock out of respect to the man who took them in.

Frank won the UFC middleweight championship and retired from the UFC undefeated after defending his title four times. He's considered pound for pound the greatest UFC fighter of all time.

But that wasn't the end of his fighting career. He's been an announcer for the UFC, he owns a chain of fighting schools, and he's gone on to train some of the greatest fighters ever. He's giving back what he was taught.

I met Frank a few years ago. He told me his secret to being the best fighter in the world. In fact, he said, this is the secret to being among the best in anything you want: Plus, Minus, Equals.

PLUS

Get a good mentor. For Frank, it was his adopted father, Bob Shamrock, and then his adopted brother Ken Shamrock.

If you don't have a mentor, get a virtual mentor. Get many virtual mentors. "Plus" is all of your mentors, virtual mentors, any person you can learn from. When I was first learning investing, I was horrible. It was only when I sat down and read everything I could about Warren Buffett that I started to get a sense of the nuances of investing.

How do you find a mentor? Sometimes I get emails from young people who are just starting out in their careers as entrepreneurs, or investors, or writers, or whatever. They say to me, "Is there anything I can do for you?"

The answer is always "No!" And sometimes their response is "Well, it doesn't hurt to ask."

It does hurt to ask. When you say to someone "What do you need?" you're giving them a homework assignment. Once I graduated high school, I didn't need any new homework assignments. I'm grateful when someone helps me, but it's hard enough having a balanced life without additional assignments like figuring out what I need help in.

Whenever I had a mentor in life, I would "overpromise and overdeliver." In college I became obsessed with being a computer programmer. I told one of my professors he should write a book. I started religiously taking notes in his class and rewriting them in his voice so he could eventually have material for a book on the topic of the class. He became my first mentor. Not because I asked but because I delivered.

When I wanted to get better as an investor, I first wrote to many people asking if they could meet me so I could pick their brains. Nobody wants their brains picked. Instead, I had to take a step back and come up with solutions for all the people I wanted to meet. Some met me and some didn't, but out of that I found several mentors. In every area of life where I wanted success, I had to find real mentors and virtual ones.

How do you find virtual mentors?

Have you ever been asked, "If you could pick any superpower, what would it be?" People come up with stupid answers like "super strength" or "flying."

Let me tell you something: if you are flying and people see you, you're going to get shot down. And exactly what are you going to do with super strength? How often do you really need to lift a car?

Reading is the most important superpower. It turns you from a normal mortal civilian into a supernatural vampire.

Someone might spend thirty years of their life developing a skill and then share the knowledge learned in those thirty years by writing a book. If you read the book carefully, take notes, reread, repeat, then it's as if you are absorbing thirty years of that person's life into your mind.

Reading lets you absorb not just one life but thousands. You have all the memories and even some of the skills of every author of every book you've read if you go through the process of reading carefully, taking notes, rereading, repeating. Reading turns every author into a virtual mentor and, trust me, virtual mentors are sometimes even better than real-life mentors.

Virtual mentors will never resent your success as you pass them by.

MINUS

My favorite quote from Albert Einstein is "If you can't explain something simply, then you don't understand it." Your "minus" is someone with fewer skills than you that you can teach. Because if you can't teach the basics so a beginner can understand, then it turns out you don't yet fully understand them yourself.

Why is Albert Einstein the first name that comes to mind when we try to think of the smartest person of all time? Why don't we think of his peers who helped him with the general theory of relativity that made him famous—Michele Besso and Marcel Grossmann? Both were talented mathematicians and physicists.

I can't answer for sure. Einstein had a certain charisma. Whether it was the hair or his eccentricity—who knows? But my guess is this: while Besso and Grossmann were great mathematicians and probably helped Einstein put together the final details of his proofs, Einstein is the one who would ask the simple questions and describe the easy-to-understand thought experiments that helped the general public comprehend his immensely complicated theories.

Einstein wondered, what if he was running as fast as a beam of light—what would he see?

It was this ability to grasp things almost in the language of a child that captured the world's imagination and transformed him from obscure physicist to celebrity genius and led him to the Nobel Prize and many other achievements. An entire mythology developed around his intelligence.

When Einstein examined a complicated mathematical theory, he always boiled it down to simple elements that he could explain to anyone. When his beliefs were shaken by quantum mechanics, a branch of physics requiring the most complicated understanding of math, he used a simple but powerful analogy to express his objections to quantum mechanics in one sentence: "God does not play dice."

José Capablanca was the world chess champion from 1921 to 1927. In 1921, he wrote a book called *Chess Fundamentals*, teaching the very basics of chess. Why, in his first year as world champion, did he write that book and not a more esoteric book analyzing the critical games that made him the best in the world?

As soon as he became world champion, he understood the importance of reminding himself of the basics. In fact, unlike the authors of the many chess books that stress understanding long and complicated variations, Capablanca wrote very simply and stuck to the basics, making his book very easy to read. He even says in a later version that the book was universal when he wrote it and would be "universal one hundred years from now." And now, exactly one hundred years later, I can tell you he is right.

Always reminding yourself of the fundamentals is the key to continued success.

Throughout Frank Shamrock's career, he's trained some of the top professional mixed martial artists, including several who made it into the top ten in the world. He was fully a master when he was able to teach and train the next generation.

When I met Frank I offered to fight him but he turned me down. Maybe one day.

EQUALS

When Frank was rising up in the UFC and mixed martial arts worlds, he would fight, train, trade notes with, and learn from his equals.

They were all rising together. With your equals, you learn by competing with them; you learn by each trying to outlearn the other, challenge the other, or impress the other. You can't do that with your mentors—they already know what you need to know—but you can do that with the people who are in your "scene."

Think of other "scenes" in history. The Homebrew Computer Club in 1970s Silicon Valley brought together a group of equals that were all interested in studying a new technology: the microcomputer. Some of them were teenagers, some a bit older, but they all spoke the language of computing and all learned from each other. Steve Jobs and Steve Wozniak were just a few of the members, and even Bill Gates and Paul Allen were known to have attended meetings.

The Beat writers formed another scene. Allen Ginsberg, Jack Kerouac, and William S. Burroughs were a few Beat writers that catapulted to fame.

Jasper Johns, Robert Rauschenberg, John Cage, and Merce Cunningham all spent time together in the 1950s as they were developing their unique styles of abstract expressionism, experimental music, and new styles of dance.

Nobody can get to the top 1 percent of a field on their own; they must find their scene. Patrick Henry may have said, "Give me liberty or give me death," but he would have been all alone if he didn't have Alexander Hamilton, James Madison, George Washington, John Adams, and others forming the scene that led to the American Revolution. And often members of your scene also become your brutal competitors, but that is part of the challenge as well—to keep pace with your equals and even pass them before they pass you.

Not all life is a competition, but we each want to flourish. And the way we can compare where we are in the hierarchy of whatever it is we are trying to learn—and every area of life has a hierarchy—is by comparing our progress with those on or near the same level in the hierarchy.

CHAPTER 8

WHO ARE YOU? WHY ARE YOU? WHY NOW?

Einstein was the ultimate outsider in the world of physics. He barely got his PhD. No university would hire him to be a professor. The best he could do was get a job at the Swiss patent office. His title: assistant examiner–level III.

Being an outsider was the greatest gift the world gave him. Rather than being swept up in university politics—who would get published, who would get tenure, who would get the best classes to teach—he was left to wonder and to think.

He started to wonder what it would be like to be in a race against a beam of light. What would the light look like? What would you look like to the light? Four years after starting his job in the patent office, he published his first research on special relativity. Unencumbered by the ambitions and problems of others, he was able to explore and to play. Suddenly this outsider became the greatest physicist of all time.

Being an outsider forces you to look at alternative routes to get to the front of the line. You see the people standing on line and, at first, you wonder why you can't stand with them. They seem content; they seem like they are friends with each other and they are moving toward that final destination together. You sense that if you were not an outsider, then perhaps you could join the line and make friends with the others who have similar interests and goals.

But this isn't going to happen.

With careers, industries, interests, and passions changing in our chaotic world, who can afford to stand in a slow-moving line while their hopes and dreams are on hold?

When Lucille Ball was fourteen, she began studying at the John Murray Anderson–Robert Milton School of Drama in New York City. She was from rural New York, but her family had moved all over the country, including spending time in Montana and in Trenton, New Jersey. The other students at the drama school laughed at her country mannerisms, and the teachers did not hesitate to tell her how awful she was.

You aren't good at acting, at dancing, at singing, and you're not even funny, they would tell her. Lonely for her mother and other companions, she shrank into herself and became too introverted to perform.

It was the Great Depression and, in order to succeed, she began accepting modeling jobs to make money. She tried to be a showgirl but was fired because she couldn't dance. Finally, she got bit parts in Hollywood movies, but for years she couldn't break out.

Eventually, she started to get noticed in a radio show, *My Favorite Husband*, on which she played a housewife. CBS wanted to develop it for television. She wanted to do it but with one catch—she demanded that they cast her real-life husband, Desi Arnaz, as her husband.

They refused to do it. They didn't think that the American public would believe that her character would be married to a Cuban.

Being on the outside was nothing new to her. And being told "You can't do that!" was all she had heard her entire time trying to make it big in show business. So she and Desi Arnaz tried a little experiment.

They performed a vaudeville act of what would eventually become their show *I Love Lucy*. It was a hit and CBS agreed to do it as a television show. It was the number one show in the country for four of the six seasons that it ran, and when it stopped after 180 episodes, it was the first show ever to stop at the top of the ratings. (Only two others did afterward—*The Andy Griffith Show* and *Seinfeld*.)

Ernest Hemingway wrote that life is a movable feast: it shifts and twists in unexpected ways. Every time I sold a company, I thought that I had finally forced life to conform to my wishes and that my need for improvement was over. It was exactly at these moments that I would always go broke. And then I would have to find that feast again.

The movable feast will leave without notice, and what will replace it will be a feeling that nobody is on your side. The world will feel lonely and dark. It is in these moments that you need to be able to answer these questions: Who are you? Why are you? Why now? These three questions unlock the self-awareness you need to flourish in this new and unfamiliar environment.

I sometimes look back and regret that I didn't understand this earlier. It's easy to say, "Well, it all worked out for the best," or "It was meant to be," but that doesn't feel good at those moments when I feel rejected and dejected, when the world I thought I knew and understood slips into darkness.

Lucille Ball understood, after years of experience, not to count on the good graces of others to fulfill her inner passions. She conducted experiments that would shape her entire career. We don't know how many experiments she tried, but we know about the ones that created *I Love Lucy* and catapulted her beyond the "You can't do that!"

messages she heard from her teachers, her parents, Broadway produc-ers, and even CBS.

Albert Einstein removed himself completely from the whims of oth-ers so he could focus on his creativity until he was ready to share the results of his thought experiments with the world. Rather than paying attention to those who would be perfectly happy to reject him, he focused his creativity until the question "Why now?" was ready to be answered.

🔻 🔻 🔻

You will have more than one purpose in your life.

In the "ancient days," way back in the twentieth century, people would follow the straight and narrow path: school, college, job, rise up in that job, save money, retire with the gold watch, die.

This was the philosophy of "corporatism." Find your lane, stay in it, drive at a reasonable speed without any accidents, get to your desti-nation, and be nice to all of the authorities along the way.

I visited LinkedIn's offices a few years ago. I asked how many job searches were related to the gig economy. "Hardly any" was the answer. "But they are growing exponentially every year." When we reached near the highest levels of unemployment in U.S. history in 2020, almost everyone I spoke to asked me if I had some fun ideas for side hustles. In fact, so many people were asking this that I ran an experiment.

In addition to my usual one- to three-hour podcasts that I release three times a week, I decided to do a new mini-podcast called "Side Hustle Fridays." It would run just five minutes every Friday and de-scribe a quirky gig or side hustle that someone might want to pursue. It was an experiment, and it took me only a half hour to record the first few, which would be enough to test out if it would be popular. Each episode had double the traffic of the prior one. Then I found sponsors for those five-minute episodes. That experiment worked.

As an employee of a large corporation, you can learn valuable lessons about the industry the corporation is in: You can learn how large corporations are managed and what might be good management versus bad management. You can learn how to succeed (or fail) in a highly structured environment. These are not bad lessons to learn, and these skills might help you borrow hours in a new pursuit. But in most cases, you don't have a chance to succeed in the things you are passionate about. You learn to do what's required to get ahead, but that's not the same. Sure, you might be able to evolve into an "entreployee," be very entrepreneurial within the corporation, blaze your own path, and find success in accordance with what the corporation values. But the average employee is usually a cog in the machine, never really sees the bigger picture, and often confuses the purpose and vision of the corporation with their own purpose. This denies the employee the opportunity to find their own vision and create their own impact on the world.

Again, there are always exceptions.

Some corporations are breeding grounds for innovation. Steve Chen was once at a dinner party with his friend Chad Hurley. They took some videos of the party and wanted to share those videos with friends. They realized it wasn't so easy to store a video and easily share it in a common format that would be accessible to everyone. Flickr, a photo-sharing site (later acquired by Yahoo!) converted every photo to a standard format so people could share photos simply by uploading them to Flickr and then sharing the link with friends. Why not a video-sharing site that operates the same way?

Often an idea that works well in one domain will work well in another (see chapter 10: "Learn Idea Calculus").

They created YouTube, which they sold less than two years later to Google for $1.65 billion.

Steve Chen wasn't working in isolation in a garage. He was fortunate enough to work for PayPal, founded by Peter Thiel and Elon Musk.

PayPal made it very easy, regardless of what type of computer or mobile device you had, to make payments from one device to another. This created the entire industry of digital payments. The company was constantly pivoting and always remained entrepreneurial. Former employees of PayPal (like Chen) quickly became known as the PayPal Mafia. The company was a great breeding ground for future success. Here are a few of the companies that ex-employees of PayPal created:

- LinkedIn, founded by Reid Hoffman
- Yelp, started by Russel Simmons
- Reddit, started by Steve Huffman and Alexis Ohanian
- Palantir, started by Joe Lonsdale
- Yammer, founded by David Sacks

All of these ideas became billion-dollar companies. Did their founders benefit because they all networked together? That was part of it. But they also benefited by seeing that Peter Thiel and Elon Musk's vision went beyond PayPal. Their vision was that soon all everyday activities (video sharing, restaurant reviews, résumé sharing, corporate communications, etc.) would find their way onto the internet.

Feeding off that vision, and learning from their founders' aggressive, adaptive approaches, these "entreployees" became entrepreneurs themselves, creating their own visions on top of the vision and purpose they learned from PayPal's founders.

Corporatism by itself is often the opposite of entrepreneurialism.

Unless you continue to grow, learn, be curious, and ultimately surpass the initial vision you subscribed to when you joined a corporation, you won't be guaranteed much beyond a paycheck, and even that is a tough bet to make these days. That's why it's more important than ever, and frankly more fun, to speak with your own voice. A voice that will shake the world.

Your purposes are spread out throughout your life like a bunch of clues in a scavenger hunt. There are multiple ways to win, but you won't win—that is, find your purpose—if you don't push forward and continue looking for the clues.

Again, there's no one purpose in life. There are many. And you can't wait for purpose to come to you. You can't think your way to purpose either.

I get emails almost every day from people who tell me, "I'm eighteen (or I'm twenty-seven . . . or I'm sixty-one . . .) and I haven't found my purpose in life yet. Am I a failure?"

Of course not.

You have to do things. You have to try. Doing > thinking. And experimenting is the best way to *do*.

Obsession is the first clue toward finding your purpose. And *doing* helps you find what you are obsessed with.

I have spoken to hundreds of people who have found their purposes—everyone from Richard Branson to Tyra Banks to race car driver Danica Patrick to former world chess champion Garry Kasparov to writers Ken Follett and Judy Blume to self-help gurus Tony Robbins and Wayne Dyer and many more.

First, all of them had some version of a daily practice to help them improve 1 percent every day. What are the essential types of components of a daily practice?

- Physical: Eat, move, sleep. If you're in bed sick, then a purpose will do you no good.
- Emotional: Trim the toxic people (even if they are "friends" or family) and be with the people who love you and support you and whom you love and support. If you are constantly angry or resentful or nervous about your relationships, your purpose will forget you.
- Mental: Exercise your creativity muscle every day. If you aren't creative every day, the muscle will atrophy. And if you are creative every day (just write down ten ideas a day on a pad), it will become a creativity superpower. Without that superpower, you will have no chance of finding a purpose and then exceeding what's been done before. Find your own unique voice that will make you rise above everyone else.
- Spiritual: Surrender to the things you cannot control. Not in a prayer sense (although it could be). Not in a meditation sense (although it could be). Not in an "angels" sense (OK, it won't be that). It's a feeling that you can't control everything. Only focus on the things within your control. Have no anxiety or regret or resentment about what you can't control.

I do this daily practice every day to keep my foundation strong and active. Without it, there's no way to find purpose. If I don't do it, within a week or so the first thoughts of depression, anger, resentment, or worse start to take hold.

You don't want the building to collapse.

Second, remember that you have more than one purpose.

I spoke to Tony Hawk, National Skateboard Association champion for twelve years. Now retired, he makes the best video games for skateboarders.

I spoke to Garry Kasparov, former world chess champion for nineteen years and still one of the best chess players in the world. Now he uses that platform to fight for human rights all over the world.

I spoke to entrepreneur Arianna Huffington. She wanted a platform to share news that was more accurate and powerful than traditional news sources. She created the Huffington Post, which became a platform for thousands of writers to share ideas and news and begin their writing careers. It was one of the first attempts at using the internet to break free from traditional news sources. She showed that the internet didn't have to be an anonymous group of trolls shouting opinions into cyberspace, but that legitimate journalism could occur.

She sold the Huffington Post to AOL for $315 million. Later, she became obsessed with the relationship between sleep and health. She writes books about sleep and that has morphed into her new organization, Thrive Global, which seeks to cover the relationship between stress and health.

I asked Danica Patrick, the highest-ranking female race car driver, how she thinks about finding a purpose, first when she was still racing professionally and now that she's retired at the age of thirty-eight.

She told me three of her ideas:

1. Ask yourself, "How would I structure the ideal day?"

2. What photos are on your phone? The thing you take the most photos of might contain a clue to your purpose.

3. What makes you most energized? List everything you did this past month, and then rank them by how happy you were when you were doing each activity.

These all lead to clues about your purpose.

Let me add one more:

> 4. What were you most interested in from ages twelve to fifteen? How have those interests aged?

For instance, if you loved basketball as a teenager, you might now, at age fifty, want to write a blog about basketball, or start a fantasy basketball league, or maybe be a basketball coach, or write a book, or make clothes for basketball, or maybe make music for basketball teams.

Jesse Itzler was a failed rapper. He loved rap, but his songs just wouldn't break out (look on YouTube for Jesse Jaymes, "College Girls").

But interests age and change as we get older. Jesse wasn't making it as a rapper. In part because of another rapper, Vanilla Ice. So instead, Jesse started making songs that sports teams could use as their anthems during games.

He built that business and sold it.

Then he flew on a private plane. He thought, *This is amazing! But more people should have access to this.* So he created Marquis Jet, a service that allowed for people to fly on private jets without actually owning a jet. He sold that to NetJets, owned by Warren Buffett's Berkshire Hathaway.

But old interests don't just go away. Now Jesse is back to his interest in sports. He doesn't play basketball, but he does *own* the NBA's Atlanta Hawks, and after starting his career with zero dollars in the bank.

Matt Berry was a Hollywood screenwriter. That seems like the dream job. But he was sick of it.

He quit his job, lost everything, got divorced, and after he had been making a good income writing movies in Hollywood, he started to make $100 per blog post.

What was he blogging about? Fantasy sports. He loved sports as a kid. But he wasn't going to be an athlete. And there were already many successful writers and commentators on sports in general.

The way his interest aged is that he became obsessed with fantasy sports. He combined that with the skills he built up writing movies and soon he started to get a large following.

Now he's a fantasy sports anchor at ESPN. He created his own job. He was the first fantasy sports anchor in the world. When walking in the street with Matt, every other person stops us and says, "Hey, thanks for the fantasy sports tips last week!"

He found his passion, monetized it, and achieved fame from it. He found "the room least crowded." And all this despite the fact that he started later in life.

Fourth, practice "purpose sex." That is, mix things that you love together. If you love music and you love sports, what about music for sports teams? See the Jesse Itzler example on the previous page.

If you love psychology and you love economics, what about creating the field of behavioral economics and then winning the Nobel Prize like Daniel Kahneman?

If you love media and you love astronomy, be like Neil deGrasse Tyson and create books, shows, and podcasts that explain astronomy to laymen.

Finally, figure out what you're afraid to do. Fear is a compass.

Without that fear, you know that you are just repeating what others have done before you. That's why, instinctively, you know it's safe.

Chess players often train by studying the opening moves played by world champions before them. Often the first ten to twenty moves of a tournament chess game played by amateurs are moves they've memorized from games they've studied of the world champions. There's no fear when they play those moves, and those moves are often played very quickly.

It's only when a player has to make a move outside of what they've memorized that their hands start to shake and their heart beats a little faster. Now they are in new territory. If they are a top player, then their moves might change the entire theoretical knowledge of chess. If they are an amateur, the new moves will give them a starting point for learning when they study the game after it's over.

Only later in life do we become nervous about being curious. We become afraid of what people will think of us. Or we become afraid of appearing stupid. Or we become afraid of being exposed as the impostor we think we are.

It's worth pointing out that when you start doing your passion, you might be very unhappy. I'm sure Matt Berry wasn't very happy when he was just getting $100 a blog post. I'm sure Jesse Itzler would've preferred if his initial foray into rap music was a huge success. And I'm sure Danica Patrick has lost many races. None of that feels pleasant.

What does fear have to do with this? I'm also afraid to jump off a building, but that doesn't mean I'm passionate about it.

You have to ask what it is you are afraid of. Are you afraid that you might not be good at something you love? Are you afraid you would lose status with a group of people?

Lean in to the fear. If I write something and think to myself, *Uh oh, I hope people don't hate me after I publish this*, that has nothing to do with the writing itself or my skill level as a writer. It is a fear that I am moving the needle of my life too much. Lean in to that. Hit Publish. That's the experiment.

▼ ▼ ▼

But what do you do once you find clues to your purpose?

1. List all the ways you can spend more and more of your day involved in that purpose.

2. Find a community of people who love that purpose just like you do. Compare notes. Learn. Help people. Find mentors.

3. Read as much as you can about that purpose. Read the history. Read the biographies of the greats. Read all of the current thinking. You need to do this to discover your unique voice.

4. Have purpose sex. See page 97.

5. DO. Start doing things that make a name for yourself in that purpose.

When I got fascinated with investing in 2002, I read every book. Then I wrote software modeling the markets. Then I started sharing my results with others and they started investing with me. Then I started writing about investing (purpose sex). Then I built a website devoted to investors. Then I built businesses around investing. And, of course, I learned every strategy of investing and started investing more and more successfully.

▼ ▼ ▼

What I found when I learned these various skip-the-line techniques is that they helped me to better get into the state that behavioral psychologists call "well-being."

There's no reason to be successful at something if it doesn't also satisfy the needs and pleasures of living life, of being the best person you can in the tiny time we are allotted on this planet.

Many people are set adrift on this planet, not sure of direction, not sure where to go. It's as if they let the wind and the weather—or the passions of other people—dictate their path. It's like traveling on a boat on a foggy night: you're confused and scared and not sure where the destination is.

The times when I focused on a specific goal—like money, for instance—were among the unhappiest times in my life. These were the goals that society was telling me would reward me with friends, lovers, luxuries, and happiness. I would be accepted, even wanted for my opinions and my favors. But skipping the line, taking a passion, and leaping into the top 1 percent of that pursuit is outside the rules of the conventional world. The conventional world will never allow you to take this leap, and it will try to convince you every second of the day of the mistakes you are making. But you only have one life—what if you spend that entire life believing these myths? What if they are coming from people who all have your best interests at heart? But never forget that it is *their* hearts and not yours where their good intentions, the myths they choose to live by, are residing.

You have to reclaim your intentions and your awareness of yourself from all who will try to convince you that your best interests are aligned with theirs. And they might have good intentions. Why wouldn't they? But nobody I have ever known has ever woken up and said to themselves, "I can't wait to make James Altucher a huge success today."

In every tribe or hierarchy I've ever been in, I've had to wear the masks and costumes of that tribe in order to be accepted. I've had to live according to their customs and rituals. Whether it was going to work in a suit in the corporate world, or playing the role of smart investor in the finance world, or letting my own insecurities cater too much to the whims of people I wanted to be in a relationship with because I was too afraid the other person wouldn't like the "real me."

It is a huge delusion that "in order to get along, you have to play along." It is only when you take off those masks and costumes and throw away the mirrors society puts before you that you suddenly wake up and decide which paths are the ones that have been ready for you all along.

In 2010, after nine years of having money as my primary pursuit, I was tired of being unhappy all the time. Tired of being anxious about me. Tired of being scared I would never have any purpose in life, never get good at anything, never find a community of like-minded people. Tired of constantly being worried about going broke. I was slowly getting more and more depressed, more and more anxious.

I wanted my ideas to work. I wanted to improve in life. I wanted that sense of contentment that I saw in others but not myself. I wanted to live a life in which I was satisfied with the people and things around me, not constantly striving for a mindless more.

Basically, I gave up. I quit. I surrendered.

We often think of life as a giant experiment in social Darwinism: survival of the fittest. And even now, during periods of recession or depression, we often think that the ones who avoided bankruptcy and despair are the "fittest" and worthiest of moving on to the next generation of economic success.

When I was at that low point more than ten years ago, I was thinking that maybe all along I was the "weak" one. Before then, since I was a kid, I had always thought that I had some potential, that I was smart and destined for easy success.

When I would go broke, then make back the money, then go broke again, and again, and again, and again, I couldn't understand it.

One time, just after I had gotten divorced, I was alone in a motel and the Great Recession was raging on the TV, with every stock red. I was losing my home and nobody was returning my calls. Again.

How could this be happening to me? I was like a lawyer and the person on the stand all at once: "You are guilty!" I was both my accuser and the guilty suspect. I felt guilty for being weak, for squandering whatever false abilities I thought I had. I'd see handsome, successful billionaires trotting out on TV, trying to explain the economics of the world so that the little people could understand. I wanted to be one of them. But there I was in a motel room. Lonely.

I remember going to sleep not because I was tired but because there was just nothing for me to do and nothing for me to be excited to be awake for. I'd just try to sleep for as long as possible so another day could go by.

But I couldn't sleep. I kept challenging the notion of survival of the fittest. Does it mean only the people who are willing to stomp on the weak and powerless in order to get ahead can win?

Of course not, I thought. There's something wrong with this.

What if the frame was incorrect? What if it's not survival of the fittest but survival of the "well-est"? If someone was content with their life and figured out how to consistently feel that contentment, what could bring them down? If someone could check the boxes on all the things that made them feel satisfied with their lives, then would they ever fall into despair?

So I conducted an experiment. Every time I felt resentment toward others that seemed "happier" (whatever "happiness" means) or any time I felt guilt over my own lack of success and regret over consistently going broke, I'd remind myself that social Darwinism was not as brutal and ruthless as I once thought and that survival depended on who could consistently tap into well-being.

But what is well-being?

In addition to the daily practice I described earlier, with a focus on physical, emotional, mental (creative), and spiritual health, the components of well-being that I've noticed in myself and many of the people I've interviewed over the years have boiled down to three factors. I haven't done a scientific study. But even without that, it's easy to see that the factors below also contribute to success in skipping the line, no matter what area or industry that line is in.

1. Community: Connecting with other like-minded people who are not toxic and care about each other's success. Ask at the end of each day: What did I do to nourish the relationships of those closest to me?

2. Improvement/mastery: The exquisite pleasure of moving up the learning curve and achieving more mastery in the areas you love. Ask at the end of each day: What did I improve at today? What new things did I learn? What new curiosities were created by my activities today?

3. Freedom: Nobody telling you what you can't do and doing the things that you love without fear. As you master more than one hierarchy, you can switch back and forth between interests and pursuits so that you spend more and more of your day making decisions that are your choice and nobody else's. How can you measure freedom? Always ask: What percentage of decisions did I make today that were completely my own and not just the thinking of a boss, a parent, a teacher, a peer, etc.?

I can choose these three factors for myself every day. Nobody has to give them to me. And nobody can take them. I can cultivate them in my actions, in my beliefs, in my treatment of others and myself. Checking these boxes each day I remain in this life reminds me once again that I've survived. Survival of the "well-est."

CHAPTER 9

EXERCISE THE POSSIBILITY MUSCLE

I don't like to feel horrible.

But if you throw your whole life into something, sometimes you will succeed and sometimes you will fail.

When I fail, it feels horrible. Of course, I will try to learn from failure. Of course, failure can propel one to success.

But it feels like death.

This is for reasons described earlier. You find your subculture, your new tribe that shares your passion. When you start to begin on that learning curve, you're going to fail a lot.

There are two types of failure:

- Omission: If you don't try at all, then you've failed. Particularly if it's something where all the clues suggested you could potentially be passionate about it.
- Commission: You go up onstage, write that novel, drive that race car, come up with that business idea, and you lose, or people don't like it, or you lose money, or you lose the race.

Only failure of omission is real failure. Because if you don't *do* something, you can't learn from your experience. Every experience is a teacher, filled with enough lessons to carry you to the next level of your education in any field.

Again, the habit of constantly experimenting in all facets of your life will bring you enormous success. With each experiment you are either adding to your knowledge or you are succeeding and propelling forward in the hierarchy of that interest/passion/career.

But . . .

When I invest in myself, I make sure I diversify. The easiest way to avoid that cortisol spike when it feels like you are getting kicked out of the tribe is to switch to another tribe, another hierarchy. This is the benefit we have now as humans that no other animals, or people at any other time in history, have had.

When one thing is not going so well for me, I switch to other interests I am passionate about.

There are many benefits to this. Sometimes excelling in another pursuit will give you ideas for your initial pursuit. Also, you might get the dopamine hit that gives you energy to go back to the passion you were not doing as well in. And it clears your head so you can rejuvenate, rest, and begin your experiments again with new creativity, new ideas, fresh energy.

It's not always possible to be happy all the time, but it is possible to strive for contentment and well-being as much as you can.

❧ ❧ ❧

The world is often put into crisis. When soldiers returned from World War II, everything was different. Alliances that had lasted for decades were now shifted. What would the world start to turn into? How would it look? The world was filled with possibility but also uncertainty.

It felt the same after 9/11. What would happen? Were we in a "new normal" that would cause us to be afraid every time an airplane flew overhead?

And what about the financial crisis of 2008? Would we be afraid to buy homes? Would the banks collapse and leave us with no way to dig out of the mess?

After the pandemic/economic lockdown, the world didn't seem to have a new normal. It was more like a new abnormal. Or what I like to call "The Great Reset," as too many things in society began to change to even suggest we were close to returning to normal.

I was afraid. At first I told myself I was afraid for the sake of my children. I wanted them to grow up in the status quo, in a normal that resembled the normal I grew up in. Although the cloud of "mutual assured destruction" from nuclear attacks seemed to hang over our heads as kids many years ago, it still seemed like it would never happen and that life, in general, would be fairly smooth.

Suddenly I wanted to cling to certainty in the middle of all this uncertainty. I found myself arguing on Twitter. *There's someone upset at me on Twitter!* And I would respond and respond. *I must convince everyone that the world will be OK. That things will return to normal.*

But I was the one who was scared. I was afraid of any change that could result. I wanted to find something, anything that I could hold on to that would show me that the world we would enter on the other side of this dark tunnel would resemble the world we left.

But the world, even day to day in what we would consider a "normal world," is never truly normal. Every day the possibilities around us shift and change. The people who see the world in terms of shades of possibility won't get lost as these possibilities change. Everyone else may be clinging to the trees to avoid flying away in a tornado, but the person who leans in to possibility gets sucked into the tornado, learns to fly, and might just land in that magical Land of Oz where not only is everything possible, everything is doable.

⬇ ⬇ ⬇

My first idea list was the table of contents for a book I wanted to write. The book was going to be called *How to Beat Your Friends and Family at Every Game in the Universe.*

For every game, I'd write three tips that, if you just knew those tips, would allow you to beat anyone who was just a casual player.

For instance, for Scrabble: learn all the two letter words. Like "xu," "qi," "za," etc. Also learn the *q* without *u* words. Like "qat," "qoph," "qanat," etc.

For Monopoly: buy the orange properties. Because the most landed on square is Jail and since the average dice roll is 7 you are very likely to end up on one of either St. James Place, New York Avenue, or Tennessee Avenue.

I was depressed and jobless and careerless at the time. I needed new possibilities in my life. But I couldn't figure out what was possible.

The world of possibilities is the same as the world of ideas. If you look around and all you see is what's lacking, scarce, or failing, then your possibility muscle (I also call it the idea muscle) has atrophied.

You need to exercise it. You only see the world of possibilities if you can exercise that idea muscle every single day.

I've written about the idea muscle in previous books, but here I am going to go into it far deeper than ever before. I've never fully described how much I use the idea muscle, or what I now call the possibility muscle, in every area of my life and what techniques I specifically use to generate new ideas. Here I will.

In 2002, at the absolute depths of my depression—the worst I've ever felt in my life—I bought a box of one hundred waiter's pads for $10 at a restaurant supply store. I don't know why I bought them. I liked how they looked. I liked that a pad could fit in my pocket. I liked that they were cheap. The waiter's pads felt nostalgic to me. They made me think of diners, milkshakes, pastrami on toast, and black coffee. Everyone always rolls out their expensive and empty Moleskine notebooks at meetings. I keep it plain and simple with my waiter's pad.

I needed to figure out what to do with my life. I was losing my home. I had two kids to feed. And sometimes I was so depressed I'd stay in bed all day. I'd see people laugh and talk and hug and kiss and I couldn't understand what inner resource they had, what emotional infrastructure was still intact enough that they could create a smile out of nothing.

Until I bought these pads. Until I made that first list.

The list: chess, checkers, poker, backgammon, Othello, Go, hearts, Scrabble, Monopoly, dominoes.

The next day I wrote another list: the tips for each game. The next day I wrote the table of contents of the sequel (bridge, spades, Risk, etc.).

The next day I wrote the titles of articles I wanted to write. The next day I wrote the names of people who inspired me who I wanted to meet.

I sent emails to all of those people. I said, "I'd love to buy you a cup of coffee." Nobody responded.

And why would they? It's not like Warren Buffett (who was on my list) is sitting at his desk waiting for someone to buy him a cup of coffee.

He's not going to get my email and suddenly say, "OMG! James Altucher wants to buy me coffee. Cancel all my meetings!"

So I tried an experiment. I came up with ten ideas to improve the business of each person I wanted to meet.

Then I sent the emails again and included the ideas. I said, "I admire your work and here are ten ideas that I think can improve your" business/writing/fund/whatever it was they did.

Of the twenty people I wrote to, three responded. (I've found this to be the correct ratio of responses over the years.) One of them was a writer. I said, "I love your writing and here are ten ideas that I would love to read your perspective on."

Nothing else. I didn't ask for anything. I sincerely thought these would be great articles for him to write.

He never wrote those articles. Instead, Jim Cramer wrote back to me and said, "I love these! How about you write them?" And this started me on a writing career at Jim's company and then expanded to writing for the *Wall Street Journal,* the *Financial Times,* and eventually authoring more than twenty books.

I had a new career as a writer.

Another person was a hedge fund manager (a professional investor). I had written ten investing ideas for his hedge fund. He wrote back and invited me to lunch. Then we went to dinner. Then he invested money with me.

I had a new career as a professional investor.

There was one person I didn't respond to. He wrote to me and said, "Let's go to lunch." Twelve years later I finally hit Reply to his email and said, "OK," as if I was responding immediately to his email from twelve years earlier. "But instead of lunch, come on my podcast." And he did. This was a three-second experiment (replying "OK" to an email twelve years later) that worked.

But after this first round of idea generation and the beginning results of me building up the idea muscle, something started to happen.

I was no longer depressed. I was writing down ten ideas every day. I started in June 2002. By September 2002 I felt like my brain was on fire. I couldn't wait to get up, get to a café, read for a little bit, then start writing down my ideas.

Ten ideas a day.

Business ideas. Book ideas. Article ideas. Ideas for other people, other businesses. If I had a business idea from the day before that I liked, then I would write ten ideas on how to create that business.

Then I started writing down "Ten Ideas for Amazon." "Ten Ideas for Google." Even "Ten Ideas for Quora."

I would share them with the companies. I stopped caring whether someone would steal my ideas. I was *abundant* with ideas. Steal away!

Because of those lists, and because I would try to share them with the companies I was writing about, I've now visited Google (I did a "Talks at Google"), LinkedIn (I spent a day consulting), Facebook, Quora, Airbnb (I spoke at the 2016 Airbnb Open), Twitter, and many other companies.

The world opened up. Now I look around and I see possibilities. When you rewire your brain like this, all you see are possible futures for yourself. And they are abundant.

Eighteen years later I still write down ten ideas every single day.

In the middle of the pandemic crisis, I wrote "Ten Business Ideas for the 'New Normal' After the Covid-19 Crisis Dies Down." I also wrote "Ten Ideas for TV shows for Disney+." I emailed the ideas to Disney. I had a friend who worked there. He forwarded the list to his friend who forwarded it to his friend, and the next thing I knew I was on the phone with executives at Disney+ pitching my ideas.

This is the magic of writing down ten ideas a day. You become so abundant with ideas you have no problem sharing them. And sharing them will create new opportunities, new connections, new worlds that will open up for you.

Starting around September 2002, I realized the key: it doesn't matter if the ideas are good or bad or if I keep track of them or if I ever look at them again.

Writing down ten ideas a day was rewiring my brain. It was giving me a dopamine boost and the feeling of achievement every morning. And then it started building up my idea muscle.

Muscles atrophy quickly. If you lie in bed for two weeks, you might need physical therapy to walk again. That's how fast leg muscles atrophy.

The idea muscle is the same way. Use it or lose it. I had lost it in early 2002. I had no creativity left in me. I was Burnt. Out.

By writing down ideas, I was exercising my idea muscle. I was connecting all the creative parts of my brain and forcing them to light up in new ways. I could feel the dusty unused parts of my brain actually begin to come to life.

And it really felt like exercise.

Every day, by the time I'd hit number seven on my list of ten, I'd keep counting over and over again: *How many ideas have I written? Is it ten?* I'd sweat out the last three.

Are the ideas good?

Not really. Hardly ever. If you write 3,650 ideas a year, maybe a hundred are useful in some way. Maybe a few are good enough to make money. Maybe one is *great*. Who knows?

The point is *not* to have good ideas all the time. The point is just exercise. Exercise that idea muscle. Then you will be more creative. Then you will know how to execute better than anyone else. You will feel abundant. Life around you will seem like just a collection of ideas to be transformed, improved upon, created.

By September 2002, just a few months after I had hit the lowest point in my life, my brain was on fire. The waiter's pads. The idea lists.

Exercising the possibility muscle had pulled me out of a despair I had never felt before and haven't felt since (although I've come close).

Within six months I had gotten my first paycheck ever for writing an article. And in those same six months I had gotten my first paycheck for making money investing another person's money.

After a year of no career, losing everything, being depressed, going broke, I now had *two* careers.

And a year after that I started a new business: a fund of hedge funds. Then two years later I started a new business, which combined my interests in writing, investing, and programming. I sold that business six months after I started it.

In the eighteen years since, every dime of money I've made has started off as a simple line on a waiter's pad. Every single dime.

If every day you force yourself to be creative, the brain rewires itself to make creativity a priority.

Too many people say, "Oh, I'm creative. When I need to be, I'll sit down and come up with a great idea."

It doesn't work that way. You have to dig the ditch before the rain comes.

Write down ten ideas a day for three months and you will feel like an idea machine. And you will feel abundant. Because you know that no matter what, you can keep generating ideas.

Do it for a year and it feels like you are a nuclear idea machine. Like you can be dropped off with no clothes and no wallet in the middle of the desert and come up with ideas to make a million dollars before you get home. Ideas for businesses, books, TV shows. Ideas for other businesses and ideas for other people have saved me so many times. They have added to my network, helped me start new careers with zero experience, helped me save my own businesses at the point when everything seemed lost.

In 2018 a friend of mine asked me to go to lunch with her. I was running late so we changed it to dinner.

She was trying to come up with ideas for what she should do with her investments. And then we started brainstorming on the various directions she could take her skills to create a new career.

I had lots of ideas for her. We talked for three hours before we even ordered our food. And a few months later we got married. I love her. It just goes to show that once you open yourself up to new ideas and surrender to whatever the outcome might be, anything is possible.

CHAPTER 10

LEARN IDEA CALCULUS

Coming up with ten ideas a day is not easy. That's 3,650 ideas a year.

Here are some techniques I use to generate millions of ideas.

IDEA ADDITION

Take an old idea, one that is big and popular. Maybe millions of people love it. Believe it. It's like a religion to them. Add something to it—often the wackier, the better.

Consider the paleo diet, the idea that we should eat like paleolithic people because that's what the human digestive system has evolved for over two hundred thousand years. Processed foods are only about one hundred years old, an evolutionary blip. Hence, the reasons for obesity, kidney failure, diabetes, and so on. Here's the addition: Paleo people didn't eat at regular intervals. They didn't eat three meals a day. So let's add something to the "diet plan" you see on websites. Today's Paleo Diet + Intermittent Fasting (how people really ate two hundred thousand years ago) = the Multiphasic Paleo Diet: eat at random intervals and vary the types of meals more frequently.

For example, sometimes eat one meal a day, sometimes four. Mix nuts, legumes, meat, and plants into every meal so nothing can be considered a "breakfast" or a "dinner."

Here's another example of "idea addition": During the lockdowns of 2020, I started doing my podcast remotely by using videoconferencing software. I started off using Zoom, which several hundred million people started using during the pandemic. It was fine, but I realized Zoom was created to handle interoffice meetings of remote workers but not really set up for podcasting. I made a list of ideas, "10 Ideas I Would Add to Zoom to Make It Better."

I was going to send those ideas off to Zoom. What's the worst that could happen? They would ignore me and the net result is that I exercised my idea muscle for the day. The best case? If they implemented my ideas, then I would have my ideal software for remote podcasting. Even better, Zoom might be so excited by my ideas and my amazing talents and genius that they would ask me to be an adviser to the company. Just as I was about to send off the ideas, I came up with a different idea. I noticed that a lot of videoconferencing software was "open source." Meaning, I could work with a programmer and we could make our own videoconferencing software and maybe even implement some of the features and compete with Zoom.

So I started to list programmers I knew, ones I trusted enough to hire. I reached out to the first one and he said, "I can't do it, but I know someone who can." He made the introduction and I spoke for about five hours with the programmer he introduced me to. He was great! As of this writing, our new podcasting/videoconferencing platform is being worked on with the ten new features from that idea list. I'm setting up the company. Now what's the best case for that idea? I build a huge new company that also makes my podcast better and enables me to host online video events. Worst case: I will have fine-tuned these ideas even further and can . . . send them to Zoom. Who knows?

That idea list turned into an experiment. There was no real downside for me to work on this, it was easy to start, and there was enormous, enormous upside. And the worst case: I learn more about how to create a videoconferencing platform from scratch, and who knows—maybe that will be useful.

IDEA SUBTRACTION

Take an idea that seems impossible to implement. Subtract the reason you can't do it—the "can't"—and see what's left that you can still work with.

(Subtraction is *money*. Trust me.)

I saw this approach work in a meeting. We were pitching a very wealthy guy. He represented a company worth more than $100 billion. We wanted his money. We wanted a lot of his money. We were hungry for money. Our desire for money was thick. He was very blunt. He was like a hammer. He sensed that money was the main reason he was in the room. He said, "Don't count on me for a single dime of money."

The guy leading the meeting on our side was smart. He did "idea subtraction." "Take money off the table," he said. "We don't want any money from you. That's covered." Then he said, "Assuming we do not need a single dime from you, would you be interested in doing a collaboration with us where we work with your team to see if this is a viable product?" The CEO of the company said, "Of course." Why wouldn't he? And suddenly we had a joint venture with a multibillion-dollar company. And, yes, that same CEO did end up backing the company with his money.

Another example: "I wrote a book but *can't* find a publisher."

That's OK. Self-publish.

Or, "I have an idea for an app but *can't* program."

That's OK. Go to Freelancer.com and for about $600 you can out-source to a good programmer.

Or, "I have an idea for a clothing line and I want it all made in America but *can't* find a manufacturer."

That's OK. Make the first samples/designs in China. See if there is a market. Then find a way to make it in America.

Once you identify what you need but *don't* have—money, time, connections—you can start to work with what you *do* have and find viable workarounds or interim steps that help you prove the concept before it's necessary to put the "can't" back into the equation.

IDEA MULTIPLICATION

Take one idea. Show that it works. And then change one item, like the location, and replicate it.

Example: Let's say I write successful advertising copy for a local dentist and the ads double his business. Now I have a track record.

I can go to dentists in every other region of the country and say, "Here's what I did for this dentist. For *x* dollars I can do it for you now."

So you take the same idea and multiply it many times. Then you can even multiply that. Sell "here's how I made a million dollars help-ing dentists" in a webinar.

"Idea multiplication" is the method for when you have a business idea that works in a specific instance and then you generalize it to "scale" the business.

Amazon is a great example of this. They sold books online. They said, "This works, so now what other product categories can we sell?" And then they took idea multiplication one step further when they realized that the technical infrastructure they'd built to handle their own business could be used by other businesses. And so Amazon Web Services was born.

IDEA DIVISION

Make an idea smaller.

For example, PayPal was initially a way for people to pay for anything they wanted by using their web browser. (Actually, originally it was for Palm Pilots but let's skip that.) Anyone using a web browser can pay for an item on any website? But this was too big. Need to divide the idea. Let's pick just one website: eBay. With its sole focus on eBay, PayPal became a monopoly (even beating eBay's internal competition) and then expanded from there to other marketplaces until PayPal was handling a significant amount of money transfers across the entire internet.

When I was building my first business, we made websites for companies. But it was hard to call any company and convince them they needed a website. We first focused on record labels and movie companies. We divided our idea down into a niche we could dominate. Suddenly we were *the* guys for the entertainment industry. We divided further. We were *the* guys for gangster rap websites. Then we expanded and did larger and larger websites.

IDEA SEX

Merge two ideas into one.

For example: the cell phone + the iPod = the iPhone.

Or, when Wyclef Jean, an already popular performer from the rap group the Fugees, combined rap with the Bee Gees song "Stayin' Alive" to make the song "We Trying to Stay Alive." He knew it would be a huge hit. Take the most popular disco song ever and combine it with a hip-hop/reggae beat and get fellow Fugees member Pras to guest on it. Heck, even I could perform that song and auto-tune my voice and it would probably be OK.

Stan Weston had an idea that would change the lives of little boys forever. And then he made a really bad decision. He knew that girls liked to play with dolls. But boys had no dolls to play with. Boys liked guns. But, he thought, action dolls + war = ?? He made a doll based on a soldier, gave it a plastic gun, and called it an "action figure." He named it G.I. Joe. He showed it to Hasbro, and Hasbro made him an offer he couldn't refuse. Hasbro said, "We'll give you a license to take a piece of revenue forever. Or we'll give you $75,000." Stan drove a hard bargain. He got them to raise that $75,000 to $100,000. He went home a happy man and put the $100,000 in his bank account. Since then, G.I. Joe has sold over $1 billion worth of merchandise. Stan Weston didn't come up with the newest newest new thing. All he did was combine the simplest concepts and make something that millions of kids loved. *This* is the critical thing he said that defined his success.

Tyra Banks was a supermodel. And she loved the TV show *American Idol*. Loved it. "It was my favorite show," she told me. Supermodel + *American Idol* = *America's Next Top Model*. Now it's a multibillion-dollar franchise syndicated into more than thirty countries and on its twenty-fifth season.

Roy Lichtenstein wanted to make a name for himself as an artist. He was a great painter, but to be known in the art world, to make money in the art world, you have to push the edge further. He was an unknown professional (barely) artist for ten years and was about to give up. He began teaching art at Rutgers University (oh, to be a fly on the wall in that class).

Then he took kitschy romance comics, blew them up, used Ben-Day dots to redraw them, and filled in the thought bubbles with his own words. (I love the one with the woman crying on the ground saying, "Oh Brad! You never called me again. Classic us!") His work *Masterpiece* sold in 2017 for $165 *million*.

So that's it. Make two lists of what people love. Combine them. Have fun.

🔻 🔻 🔻

Sometimes various skills and talents can combine as part of "talent sex" or "career sex" to create an even better career and allow someone to move faster to the top of a hierarchy.

"Talent sex" may seem like an unusual way to explain Jackie Robinson's success, but hear me out. Robinson is famous for being the first player in baseball's Negro Leagues to enter Major League Baseball. There was an unwritten rule among baseball owners to not sign someone out of the Negro Leagues. Even though many African Americans had fought for their country and risked their lives in World War II, segregation ran deep in sports. Baseball owners were also worried that if they signed a player from the Negro Leagues, it might result in people protesting their games or, worse, violence. Was Jackie Robinson the best player in the Negro Leagues? He was certainly one of the best. But another player, Roy Campanella, had better overall statistics: more experience, more home runs, a better batting average, and so on. Both were signed by the Brooklyn Dodgers, but Robinson was the first to play, making history, and his name will be linked forever with civil rights and sports.

Why was he able to skip the line?

Branch Rickey, the general manager of the Dodgers, was not only interested in recruiting the best player but also a player who would be able to withstand the racial abuse that would definitely be thrown at the player and the team. He asked Robinson about this directly, and Robinson was horrified. "Are you looking for a Negro who is afraid to fight back?" he famously asked. Rickey responded, "I'm looking for someone who has the guts to not fight back."

The principles of civil resistance that Martin Luther King Jr. so avidly and successfully advocated for to propel the civil rights movement ten years later were what Branch Rickey was looking for in sports in 1946.

And this is where Robinson had years of experience. As an officer in the military (it was itself a battle to become an officer rather than an enlisted person as an African American), Robinson, long before Rosa Parks, had refused to move to the back of the bus when he was asked to. The military tried to court-martial him, even throwing in a charge of "public drunkenness," which was false (Robinson did not drink). Robinson was able to argue his case in front of an all-white panel and the charges were dismissed. Again, he built up the skills that were later followed (accidentally or not) by Martin Luther King Jr., who proposed nonviolent resistance in the face of great discrimination and used that nonresistance to push forward all the civil rights reforms passed in the mid-1960s.

It was this combination of his political awareness, his ability to hone his emotions for a bigger cause, and, of course, his baseball skills that was the "talent sex" needed for Robinson (who had only played one year in the Negro Leagues versus Campanella's nine) to become the first African American to play in Major League Baseball, successfully integrating the sport.

◆ ◆ ◆

In 2016, I was staying with my friend Scot. I had just begun another experiment. I had thrown out all of my belongings except what I could fit in one carry-on bag. I was living out of Airbnbs for a few days at a time. I wanted to experiment with what it would be like to be a true minimalist. A nomad. Occasionally, during this period, I would stay a few days with friends around the country.

Every few days I lived at a new Airbnb. I moved around all over the world. Maybe I've stayed in more Airbnbs than anyone else. As a result I would write idea lists about how Airbnb could improve their services. I shared these ideas with Airbnb and this got me an invitation to speak at the Airbnb Open.

Then a reporter, Alex Williams, heard about my story and wrote about it for the *New York Times*. Steven Spielberg saw the article and his office reached out and wanted me to do a TV show about the experience. Will something happen? Will I have a TV show? Probably not, but I did attend several meetings and learned an enormous amount about the industry. I didn't want to attach myself to any outcome, but I put my energy into learning. It was an experiment, and no matter what happens, I learned enormously from all the meetings I've had and all the experience this experiment has led me to.

But during this period is when I stayed for a while at my friend Scot's place. While I was staying with Scot, he told me about a problem he was trying to help solve. "There are no nonlethal weapons for law enforcement," he told me. If a police force yells at a potential criminal to put their hands up and the person doesn't comply, then there are not really any safe choices for the police officer.

We were talking about this and going over ideas. He decided to call the inventor of a weapon that we had invested in ten years earlier. It was a "sonic weapon" used in the war in Afghanistan. It would shoot a highly concentrated blast of sound at a person one thousand feet away and blow them right down. If a person was standing right next to the person who heard the sound blast, they wouldn't hear it at all. That's how concentrated the sound blast was.

"Can he do this for law enforcement?" I asked Scot. He was already reaching for the phone. Scot called the inventor, but the inventor didn't think it would work. "Too close to shoot," he said. He needed it to be across farther distances.

But he had an idea.

Take traditional weapons and combine them with old-fashioned cowboy lassoing. (Idea sex!)

He invented the BolaWrap. It's a device that shoots out a Kevlar steel cable at almost the speed of sound that wraps around a potential criminal and immobilizes them. If they try to fight against the cable that is wrapped around them, the cable gets tighter. Nobody gets hurt. They just get wrapped.

Scot and I, plus a few others, were the first investors in this new company, Wrap Technologies. And we paid for the development of this new device. Four years later, the BolaWrap is used by many police agencies and is worth over $200 million on the stock market. Neither Scot nor I had any experience in law enforcement, but by investing early in this idea and connecting all the right people via "six-minute networking" (see chapter 13: "Microskills Everyone Should Learn") we went to the front of the law enforcement industry.

We did an experiment . . . and it worked. It now saves lives every day.

Combine ideas every day. Exercise the idea muscle every day. Practice makes progress. Progress makes permanent.

Pick the best idea. Make billions. Help millions. Make people happy.

Go!

▼ ▼ ▼

People say it takes 10,000 hours to become world-class.

But when I combined the concepts of financial media and social media when I made my website Stockpickr in 2007, I suddenly was the *only* person combining the two ideas. Being the only person in the room allowed me to quickly get partnerships that boosted my users into the millions, and within months I was able to sell the business at a valuation of $10 million.

I didn't need 10,000 hours. I needed to exercise the idea muscle and then do experiments to see if the idea would work. In fact, on the particular list where I wrote "social networking + financial news," that was the tenth item on the list. I tried the first nine and none of them worked (e.g., "people who smoke + dating site").

It takes 10,000 hours to be world-class at any *one* thing. It takes 1,000 hours to be world-class at an intersection. It takes 100 hours to become world-class at the intersection of three or more things. And if you use experiments to quickly try out these combinations of ideas, determining which directions will be successful and which ones won't can go even faster.

An example is the French band Gotan Project. They took an electronic beat and combined it with tango music. They've created hit after hit.

Or Scott Adams, creator of one of the most popular syndicated comic strips in the world, *Dilbert.* Instead of calling it "idea sex," he refers to this particular skip-the-line skill as a "talent stack." "I wasn't the best at drawing, but I was pretty good. I wasn't the funniest, but I was OK. And I wasn't the best at understanding the corporate world, but I was pretty good. I combined all of these and the result was *Dilbert.*"

IDEA SUBSETS

Break ideas down into parts within parts.

People say, "Execution is everything." I can tell you it isn't. If you can't come up with ideas, then you'll never be able to come up with execution ideas.

When I had an idea to create a social networking website for people interested in investing, the next thing I did was come up with "Ten Ideas for Pages on the Website." Then "Ten Things on Each Page." Then "Ten Ways I Can Execute on This." All of these were subsets of the initial idea. Two months after I developed that original list I had the first version of the website completed. Two months after that I officially announced the website. And four months later I sold the website for millions to TheStreet.com.

Many people don't understand that execution is a spectrum. You can be bad or good. The way you get good at execution is having good execution ideas. The way to get good at execution ideas is to exercise your idea muscle. When you have an idea, there are many possible ways to execute on that idea. It's like opening a mystical third eye: you can see all the possible futures and choose the best one. And how do you know which one is best? You guessed it: by experimenting.

After using these techniques for just three months, I felt as if my entire brain had been rewired. It was like seeing the world in dimensions and colors I didn't even know existed—a world colored with possibilities that were always there but that I'd never noticed before.

Here are just a few I've generated:

- 10 old ideas I can make new again (*The Wizard of Oz*, Wall Street, etc.)—similar to idea sex
- 10 ridiculous things I would invent (the smart toilet, etc.)
- 10 experiments I can do today that could lead to businesses
- 10 jokes
- 10 books I can write (*The Choose Yourself Guide to an Alternative Education*, etc.)
- 10 business ideas for Google/Amazon/Twitter/you
- 10 people I can send ideas to
- 10 businesses I can do related to coronavirus
- 10 businesses I can do related to AI or big data
- 10 online courses I can create
- 10 podcast ideas or videos I can shoot (*Lunch with James*, a video podcast where I just have lunch with people over Skype and we chat)
- 10 industries from which I can remove the middleman
- 10 things I disagree with that everyone else assumes are religion (college, home ownership, voting, doctors); or, for any one of those ideas, 10 ideas why I disagree!
- 10 ways to take old posts of mine and make books out of them
- 10 ways I can surprise my wife, Robyn (Actually, more like 100 ways. That's hard work!)
- 10 items I can put on my "10 List Ideas I Usually Write" list
- 10 people I want to be friends with and what the next steps are for contacting them (Dave Chappelle, I'm coming after you! Larry Page better watch out also.)
- 10 things I learned yesterday
- 10 things I can do differently today—write down my entire routine, from beginning to end, as detailed as possible, changing one thing and making it better

- 10 chapters for my next book
- 10 ideas for thriller novels
- 10 ways I can save time. For instance: don't watch TV, drink, have stupid business calls, play chess during the day, have dinner (I definitely will not starve), go into the city to meet one person for coffee, waste time being angry at that person who did X, Y, and Z to me, and so on.
- 10 things I learned from X, where X is someone I've spoken to recently or read a book by recently. I've written posts on this about the Beatles, Mick Jagger, Steve Jobs, Charles Bukowski, the Dalai Lama, Superman, Freakonomics, etc.
- 10 things women totally don't know about men. That turned into a list of 100 and Robyn said to me, "Uhhh, I don't think you should publish this."
- 10 more alternatives to college I can add to my book *40 Alternatives to College*
- 10 things I'm interested in getting better at (and then 10 ways I can get better at each one)
- 10 things I was interested in as a kid that might be fun to explore now (Like, maybe I can write that "Son of Dr. Strange" comic I've always been planning. And now I need 10 plot ideas.)

Developing the idea muscle is a superpower. You can be dropped off naked in the desert and use idea calculus to get back to civilization and maybe even get rich in the process.

Find that waiter's pad. Write down ten ideas a day.

CHAPTER 11

FRAME CONTROL

I was terrified that a group I was doing business with wasn't going to pay me what they owed me. I couldn't sleep. It was a big amount and I was obsessed with this. So I wanted to do a negotiation where they could pay me earlier than the scheduled date. I had gone broke so many times before it was almost like I had post-traumatic stress about getting ripped off. I couldn't function.

Another time, I was in a relationship where I didn't really understand what was happening. Why was she always mad at me? Why did I always have to defend myself when I wasn't even really sure what the underlying problems were?

In these situations, I always called a friend of mine, Bill Beteet, who is a onetime lawyer, onetime dating coach, part-time comedian. As Scott Adams, author of *Dilbert*, would say if he knew Bill, Bill has a great "talent stack" that gives him a unique perspective on persuasion. He's a pretty good lawyer, a pretty good dating coach, and a pretty good comedian. (I hope he's not upset I say "pretty good." He's actually very good at all of these, but even if he was just pretty good that would be all he needed.) The combination of these skills makes him uniquely qualified to be an expert on persuasion.

Or as he calls it, "frame control."

He explains that in every high-stakes situation, one person has the frame and the rest in the room do not. If you are a comedian, you're the one on the stage. If the audience takes the frame away from you—if, for instance, you get nervous in the middle of a joke or stumble on a punchline and don't have a quick recovery—you will never get it back and that's the end of your show. If you lose the frame in a legal case to the other lawyer, you're going to lose the case. If you lose the frame when you are asking someone out on a date, you will lose status and chances are it won't work out.

"You can't constantly control the frame or the people around you will get 'frame fatigue,'" he told me once. "But the key is to be aware of the frame so that when you need to take control of it, you can."

Over the years, I've called him to discuss many situations in my life. Together we'd walk through the situation and figure out who had the frame and who didn't and how I could make the situation work for me. Sometimes he would be so accurate it was unreal. Like if I was in an argument, he would say, "Try X, then you will see the other person do Y. Then do Z, and you will see the other person do A or B, and then you have to just be quiet and the other person will do C, and then you can do D."

"That's pretty specific," I would tell him. "Just do it," he would reply, and it would be uncanny how dead-on he was with each part of the interaction.

He and another person in whom I regularly confided, Brendon Lemon, ended up writing a book about frame control called *The Power Bible* and they came on my podcast to talk about it. Perhaps because I had used Bill's knowledge so many times over the years, they asked me to write the foreword to the book, and I used that as an opportunity to summarize many of the techniques I learned from the two of them.

Here are a few of the things I learned from them that have saved my life repeatedly.

BE AWARE OF VALIDATION VACUUMS

A validation vacuum occurs when a person who regularly validates you stops doing so. When somebody stops validating you, you will end up experiencing a myriad of emotions ranging from anger to sadness. These are all emotional states that contribute to diminishing your frame. So when you are in these states, when someone has pulled their validation from you and you are wondering if they will ever interact with you again, you will end up questioning your own frame and even making arguments against yourself. Often, you'll put yourself in a less advantageous position when the two of you reconvene. But being aware of this will stop you from experiencing the negative aspects of a validation vacuum.

KEEP IN MIND WHO HAS THE FRAME

There are some obvious ways to tell who holds the frame at any time. First, consider this: How many things are you doing to appease the person you are speaking with? Second, ask yourself: How far are you willing to go to appease this person? When you are acting in someone else's frame, you might feel strong impulses to continue a course of action that might not be to your benefit. Do a gut check. If you are starting to feel uncomfortable and/or that you're being pushed to your limit, you are most definitely in someone else's frame. Pause and gather your composure. Understand that your impulse is just a biological shortcut to keep you safe and not evidence that they are instructing you to do something that would be to your benefit. Get in the habit of asking yourself two questions in any conversation: "Am I in their frame?" and "Am I comfortable with being in their frame?" Depending on your answers, you can decide whether to stay in the frame or walk away. And if you do stay, you'll be far more difficult to manipulate.

PRIZING: OR GET OTHERS TO QUALIFY THEMSELVES TO YOU

Qualifying is the process of providing information that makes other people trust/like you. Typically, people must qualify themselves to those who hold an authority position above them. Children qualify themselves to their parents, students qualify themselves to their teachers, and employees qualify themselves to their bosses.

Now, since we typically qualify ourselves to superiors, if you get someone to qualify themselves in a conversation with you, they will start treating you like their superior. So an easy way to illicit this response from people is to ask questions that are aimed at them providing information on how they know what they know and why you should trust them.

You don't want to ask these questions directly because they will come across as rude. Rather, you want to find a way of asking these questions in a veiled capacity. When they give an answer, no matter how impressive the answer may sound, underreact. This will make the person question whether or not they are passing your "qualification process" and will make them try harder to impress you. Once you feel that you have established the power dynamic, you can switch your behavior to being a lot more warm and friendly. The validation from you becoming warm will make them forget about your icy questions at the beginning of the interaction.

None of this is done in an insincere or inauthentic way. When someone brings you new information, it's natural to want to know their qualifications. The only difference between an "expert" and an "amateur" is that the expert makes fewer amateur mistakes (hopefully). So you want to be able to assess if this information is coming from a nonamateur.

In terms of underreacting—this feels like a technique. But it isn't. At any given point, you are taking in information from a variety of sources. To give too much power to one without absorbing it and letting it sink in would be to fall under another's spell. Instead, let the information go past the initial response of your mind and see if it feels right in your heart.

SHAPING: PRAISE ANOTHER FOR A QUALITY YOU WANT THEM TO POSSESS

Have you ever noticed that if you ask someone, "Why are you getting so mad?" they quickly become upset even if they were not upset before? That's because subconsciously they are already taking on the label you have placed on them.

This technique is called "shaping," and it works in both directions. If you see someone at a party not speaking with anyone and suspect they have social anxiety and then you tell them you appreciate how their calm demeanor is making you feel more calm, they will begin to act more calm.

This is a dual-purpose weapon as it can make your allies stronger and your enemies weaker. If you want a friend to act in a particular way, just say you appreciate how they are already acting strong, calm, friendly, confident, happy, etc. If you have an enemy and want to throw them off, ask them to stop being so emotional, moody, suspicious, aggressive, passive-aggressive, anxious, etc. Remember that the emotion you label them with has to be within reason or it will sound sarcastic and dishonest.

This can work even when it's one to many. Imagine you are giving a public talk and you feel like you are losing the audience. Congratulate them on being the most attentive audience you've had in a while. Even if it comes across as a joke, guess what? They will laugh and become more attentive.

In a sales meeting, find a way to slip in, "I'm so glad you guys see the benefits of X."

And if you want, use it in your own personal life. If you feel yourself getting angry, remind yourself that this isn't the angriest you've ever been. And congratulate yourself on finding some calm in whatever storm you are in. This detaches you a bit from the events causing your emotions and allows you to take a step back, which automatically reduces the importance of these events and takes back the mental real estate you had rented out to them.

Note also, this isn't the simplistic benefit of an affirmation. Affirmations don't work if they just come from the mind. Repeating words just makes them lose their value (like everything, when supply goes up and demand remains the same, value goes down). But words that come from the heart are really just the clothes of the true impulses of what you love—these shape your mind into who you are in your heart.

TRIBE BUILDING

People are always the most suspicious of those they see as "other." A powerful strategy for gaining rapport and status is to find a common identity with those you're dealing with. We call this "tribe building."

In any situation where you know you're coming in at a lower status or having difficulty with others, find something in common and attempt to reidentify yourself to others with this quality. The beauty of this approach is that the commonality can be anything, meaningful or meaningless. To use this tactic, make a statement about a common quality or experience that's true for you and your target, then invite them to invest in that identity by confirming it or complying with it.

"We're all dealing with this weather today. You staying dry?"

"This was a rough winter for me. Was yours too?"

"Ugh! How late is this bus!?"

This tactic works because humans implicitly have different sets of rules for people in the in-group versus the out-group. However, those in-groups or out-groups are arbitrary. As soon as you establish a common identity with someone, you've formed a new tribe. Now you can lead that tribe.

In a public talk, you can pose a question to the audience like "Who here has experienced what I just spoke about?" Some people will raise their hands from one side of the audience and some will raise their hands from the other side. You can "build a tribe" by pointing to both and saying something like, "You guys need to exchange phone numbers later." People will laugh and a tribe has been built. By you.

The above examples (the weather, the late bus) might seem like small talk, but you can try this in higher-stakes situations too. When asking your boss for a raise, ask them, "What was your biggest worry when you were starting out?" If they answer, "Feeding my family," find some event in your life either now ("I know what you mean. Baby on the way.") or in the past ("My father always told me, 'Next month will be better,' and I knew it was hard for him.") that relates. Now you and the boss are in the same tribe, and again, it was you who formed it.

In his classic book *Cat's Cradle*, Kurt Vonnegut points out that many tribes are false tribes. He calls them a "granfalloon." For instance, two people who meet on a plane and realize they are both from Indiana might get excited for a brief moment but, he points out, it's not a real tribe. It's interesting to note that Vonnegut studied anthropology at the University of Chicago and so is poking holes at the concept of our need for tribes when the notion no longer exists the way it did in paleolithic times.

And yet, they are tribes. People really do get excited in a strange situation when they find any commonality at all. If a man and woman meet at a party in Iceland and realize they both lived in Kansas when they were kids, they will naturally feel that paleolithic tendency of "us versus them." Don't ignore the power of the granfalloon!

The reason sharing ideas works (see chapter 10: "Learn Idea Calculus") is that it forms an "idea tribe." If I share with the head of business development of Company X my "Ten Ideas for Company X" and my idea muscle is sufficiently well developed to have decent ideas, then the head of business development knows that I care about his advancement the way a tribe member would. We are in the same idea tribe.

Again, many people have a scarcity complex about their ideas. They feel if they share them, then those ideas will be stolen and they might never have an idea like that again.

But our value is not in the simple linear list of ideas we come up with in our lives. Our lives increase in possibility (hence the reason I often refer to the "idea muscle" perhaps more accurately as "the possibility muscle") when we grow our tribes.

When we grow our tribes, we grow not just the list of people we know in our tribe, but we also grow exponentially the number of possible connections we have in our lives and the number of possible combinations of idea sex.

If Person A is a new person in your tribe and Person A knows twenty people and you know twenty people, then the possible combinations between all the twenty people in their tribe and the twenty in yours— "Hey, I know someone who can help you. I'll introduce you."—is four hundred. Similarly, if each of those twenty have many ideas, and the twenty members of your tribe have many ideas, then the possible idea sex combinations are in the many thousands.

Tribe building becomes one of the most successful ways to expand the world of possibilities. Many people feel trapped by their particular path, as if they are locked in and can't escape. But opening up the world of possibilities opens up the world of choice. The more choices you have, the more you can choose a path that lights both your heart and mind on fire.

Tribe building is more than just small talk. It's the way to choose the best possible life for yourself.

LABELING

I want you to imagine you are talking to someone and you ask them a question. They look at you, so you know they heard it, but then they don't answer and they return to what they were doing. You feel embarrassed and want to save face, so you ask the question again. This time they do not acknowledge you at all; they just keep carrying on with their agenda. Again, you are probably feeling a mixed bag of emotions—anger, anxiety, inferiority—but one thing you're not feeling is power. You're probably not feeling seen or heard or understood. The other person has just used their power—the power of selective silence—to create a validation vacuum. They are either trying to control the frame or change it so that they don't have to answer your question.

This is your opportunity to take back the frame by "labeling" their behavior. You can say, "Did you just change the subject? How come?" Or, "Are you not answering the question for a reason?" Either way, don't let them off the hook. Don't let them change the question or the subject. Don't let them answer a different question. Always label it: "Did you just answer a different question? I'm happy to talk about the other subject, but let's stick with the original subject first."

EARNING YOUR OWN RESPECT

Others, with varying degrees of pressure, will try to take you off your path. Sometimes people do this out of habit, not out of bad faith. It is just a result of your best life conflicting with their interests.

Ironically, your ability to say no to opportunities, even good ones, is necessary to live an extraordinary life. "No" is a lot harder to say when you don't respect yourself. This is because it's easier to go along with what other people are asking you to do. You need enough self-authority to say no and even more to follow through when you do say it. Both are hard if you don't respect yourself. You also need to prepare your "no."

Ask yourself, what are your boundaries in every possible outcome of the conversation you are in. Know in advance, as much as possible, what you are willing to tolerate and what you aren't.

One quick guideline for learning to say no is to ask yourself, "If I say yes to this, will I learn something new?" If you are saying yes be-cause you are afraid of what someone else will think or you are saying yes just for the money . . . then that's the wrong reason to say yes. You must say no to those situations or be up front about the problems you are having with saying yes. People respect a well-thought-out no much more than they respect a desperate yes.

KNOW YOUR INFERIORITY NARRATIVES

Inferiority is feeling guilty for your presence. Inferiority will make you feel anxiety, a persistent worry of offending others with your presence. It's embedded in the assumption that no one likes you and that you are not worthy of other's good opinions. These self-narratives reinforce feelings of inferiority, so make friends with these stories and the self-talk you tend to use to attack yourself. Ask yourself: In the past, how have I gotten into high-stakes situations that made me feel inferior? Is this a common pattern for me?

And remind yourself: You have earned the right to be here, in this moment. Even if you are on a public stage, giving a talk, and it appears you are losing the interest of the crowd (i.e., losing the frame), remind yourself that you are on the stage because you have more experience than anyone else in the room. That's why you are there. Have a counter-story to your negative self-talk ready to assert to yourself and to others.

STEER CLEAR

When in a negotiation or an argument—or any situation where there can be only one "winner"—the person who controls the frame wins. In these situations, remaining clearheaded and unemotional is the only way to ensure that you continue to hold the frame. Actions you take in these situations must be calculated and dispassionate. This does *not* mean that you should expect to feel no emotions during a conversation that matters. It means that when you recognize that your emotions are rising, you can take action to change the frame. The simplest way to do this is to take a break or leave the negotiation/conversation temporarily—in some cases, permanently, if you can't foresee how you'll ever be able to reframe the conversation. If you must stay in the negotiation, then the negotiation is already lost—you're just working out the terms of your imprisonment.

DISRUPT THE PATTERN

When a frame shift occurs, you normally experience the shift as a change of emotion. The key to retaining or regaining control of the frame is being *nonreactive.* This is because when you react to the emotion delivered by the new frame, you are caught within that frame and have *added energy to it.* The more we react to frames, the more emotion we feel and action we take on that emotion, the stronger we make the frame we are caught in.

If you feel a change, interrupt the pattern. For instance, if you are arguing a case in court and it suddenly appears that the other lawyer is gaining ground with the jury, try a new tactic. Say your client is probably guilty. Say, "Assume he's guilty, which means you probably think X, Y, and Z." And then challenge those assumptions. Another pattern disruptor in a negotiation is to simply be silent. State what you want and don't speak. People become uncomfortable with silence and they will immediately fill the gap with words that will provide you with valuable information and allow you to regain control of the frame.

CHOOSE YOUR FRAME OR IT WILL BE CHOSEN FOR YOU

The world is interested in putting frames on you. In fact, long before you were born, the outside world determined much of your life for you. The world wants to make *you* valuable to *it*. Because of this, you must be intentional about your frame, about the frames you wish to enforce in your life. Think about how you want to act, what kind of life you want to have, the perspective you want to come from. Think about how you want to be treated. Now make the decision to have that be your frame. Go so far as to write it down and name it. Enforce this frame or the world will make you what it wants.

SPEND YOUR ENERGY WISELY

Because many people are unaware of how frames work, they mistakenly believe that taking back control of the frame involves convincing others of a different point of view. This could not be more wrong. In fact, the desire to convince comes from implicitly believing that you are less valuable than the other party. The more you try to convince another person, the more you are reinforcing the higher value of their frame. The more you put energy into persuading another, the more you are *assenting* to the placement of their frame. Instead, attempt to convince only when necessary and when you require the buy-in of others.

An argument with an anonymous stranger on Twitter, for example, is never a time to convince.

IT'S OK TO TAKE A QUALIFIED "NO"

Most people don't know why they say no to something. A danger of frame control can be the need to gain compliance or capitulation from every interaction. This is a bad frame to have and a bad way to approach interactions with others. Instead, be willing to take no as an answer from someone *as long as* they've done the required work to convince you that their no is worth taking. A good way to elicit this is to simply ask, "Can you walk me through your reasoning here?"

▼ ▼ ▼

Every negotiation, every sale, every performance or situation where the boundaries of life are being worked out involves competing frames. Do you have the frame when you are asking your boss for a raise or does your boss have the frame? Do you have the frame when you are giving a talk at an important conference or does the crowd have the frame? Do you have the frame when asking someone out on a date or is your potential date going to just ignore you and your promise of forever bliss? Understanding the basics of frame control allows you to take a step back in a high-stakes situation and ask: Who has the frame, and if not me, how do I get it back? How do I give myself the greatest odds of a good outcome here versus waiting for the outcome to happen to me?

CHAPTER 12

FIND THE CONSPIRACY NUMBER (OR HOW TO KNOW IF AN IDEA IS GOOD OR BAD)

During the quarantine, many days I'd start out thinking, *I can do anything! All of the possibilities!* And by the end of the day, I'd ask myself, *Where did the day go? How come I didn't do anything? How come I couldn't decide what activities would give me the most benefit?*

With too much wide-open space—and without a plan—I often found myself in this silent despair, knowing that the day was a gift to me but I couldn't figure out how to unwrap it. But this happens all through life, whenever we have ideas—sometimes too many ideas—without constraints and we can't figure out how to move forward.

For example, a friend told me, "I'm going to write a book. I need to make a lot of money fast or I'm going to go broke."

"OK," I said, "what are you thinking?"

He described the book to me, and it was on a topic that was very practical. People could use it to improve their lives, and he had the right combination of skills (let's call it talent sex) to make it a good book.

The only problem: he needed to make money quickly.

"This is a bad idea," I said. "Don't do it." And I described why I thought that way and what he should do instead. I was using a technique that had served me well in the past. When deciding on something, always ask, "How many things have to *conspire* to make this a good idea?" The number of things that have to conspire is the "conspiracy number."

For instance, if you want to write a book and make a lot of money from it, particularly if you have never written a book before, then:

1. You have to write the book.

2. A very good agent has to like it.

3. A publisher has to like it enough to acquire it.

4. The marketing team has to be enthused to sell it to bookstores.

5. Bookstores have to want to display it.

6. Finally, a lot of people have to buy it.

So, six things have to conspire for this strategy to work out if your goal is money. That's too many!

Even if you decide to self-publish a book, the number of things that have to conspire for you to make a significant amount of money very quickly could be too great.

1. You have to write the book.

2. You have to have a good social media platform to sell the book. (It's rare that a self-published book will sell many copies without a good social media platform.)

3. Self-published books are priced more cheaply, so you will still make about the same amount of money per book.

4. Again, you will probably have to sell 100,000 copies to make money.

I encouraged my friend to "think like a grandmaster." *Think Like a Grandmaster*, by Alexander Kotov, is a book about chess written in 1971 by one of the best players in the world. In chess, at any given point in the game, you are confronted with a variety of choices for what move to make, and then you have to determine the best move. A lot of people start off by looking for what seems like the best move and then looking at all the possible responses to that move that their opponent can make, and then all of their responses to those moves, and so on, going deep down the rabbit hole of one possible move before even considering all the other possible first moves that could have been examined. Kotov suggests a different approach, one he says the best players in the world use: go for breadth instead of depth.

First, list in your head the six to ten possibilities before looking too seriously down any one move. Then, after you've identified all the possible moves, pick one and look (with breadth) at all of your opponent's possible choices before going down any one path. And so on. List all your choices. Then start thinking. Because when you list the choices, you might see something that immediately shows you the right path. If you go too deeply down one of the choices first, you might miss the obvious and waste valuable time.

So I said to my friend, the aspiring author, let's list the choices for how you might bring your idea into the world, including publishing a book but also looking beyond that. Again, it's breadth you're looking for. (See chapter 19: "The Spoke and Wheel (or How to Monetize Anything).") Here are some of the ideas we came up with:

- A book
- A podcast
- A self-published book
- Public speaking
- Coaching
- An online course
- An online newsletter
- A for-pay Facebook group
- YouTube videos

We went down each choice and started listing the conspiracy number for each. What we settled on was an online course. What's the conspiracy number for that—not just making the course but having it make a good amount of money?

1. My friend needs to make the course: basically, each chapter in what the book would've been, a video lesson, and some exercises. He can use an already existing online platform to create the course and handle credit cards, customer service, refunds, etc.

2. If he prices high enough, he can find a distribution partner (these are called "affiliates") and do a 50/50 split to sell across their platform. For instance, he can have a discussion with someone with a big email list or a big YouTube channel and then, if they like him, they can recommend his course.

3. A valuable online course could be priced as high as several thousand dollars. For instance, one friend of mine has a course on how to get covered by the media. She charges $700. She sells about a thousand courses a year: $700,000 a year. I suggested that my friend price his course at $500 (although this can be tested). Now if he sells just two hundred courses, he makes $100,000.

That gives my friend's idea a conspiracy number of three. We went through each of the choices, and this was the lowest conspiracy number by far to get to the point where he could make $100,000 a year with a lot of upside potential.

Also, it almost qualifies as an experiment because although it would cost a tiny bit of money to produce (he needs someone to edit videos and he has to have the time to make the course), the downside is somewhat minimal, and even if the experiment "fails" (he doesn't sell enough at that price point), he can pivot models and take the ideas in the videos and turn them into a book, a YouTube channel, a for-pay Facebook group, or a trailer to pitch coaching or public speaking. Like all good experiments, this one would have little to no downside but a huge potential upside. And even in "failure" there is much to learn: he would learn how to build an online course, he would learn how to do video production, and how to employ affiliate marketing—all while developing other potential formats and uses for this very same content.

So he created his online course in about a month. He even wrote a mini-version of his book to go with it and gave that to subscribers for free. He found some people with huge social media platforms who liked his message and agreed to recommend it to their readers.

He produced the online course and made $200,000 in the first few months.

So when considering your options for which ideas to pursue and how to pursue them, you can use this approach to help you identify risks, figure out priorities, and home in on ideas with the most upside and the least downside. When trying to make a decision:

- List all the possibilities.
- Use conspiracy numbers to analyze each one. Again, how many things need to conspire for you to get to the goal you want?
- Pick the decision with the lowest conspiracy number. It should be so low that the downside/upside ratio should look like an experiment.

CHAPTER 13

MICROSKILLS EVERYONE SHOULD LEARN

As I've mentioned, you would be wise to identify the microskills you need to skip the line. If you don't know what you don't know, then how will you ever know what you need to know, you know what I'm saying? We all have our particular strengths and weaknesses, but it turns out that we share a lot of the same weaknesses. These tend to fall into the categories of communication and productivity. Here are a few techniques I've learned or developed to help me improve these microskills by 1 percent each day.

THE ADVICE TECHNIQUE

People don't like being told what to do. Ever. So I don't tell anyone what to do. I give them the freedom to decide. I call this the "advice technique." It's helped me out in hundreds of situations—from relationships to being a parent to selling a company.

If you have an idea, a perspective, a skill, or a talent and you want to translate that idea into real-world success, you have to be able to communicate it. Then you get into the realm of negotiation. Someone wants to work with you, but the stakes need to be determined. Negotiation is one of those things that people think they are automatically good or bad at. It doesn't matter what you think, the advice technique described here will make you a better negotiator.

I always thought I was a good negotiator. Looking back on it, I was horrible. Maybe the worst on the planet. This one simple idea has made me an enormous amount of money, but even more than that, it's allowed me to navigate my way through the gatekeepers that would often try to stop me from success, or try to grab too much off the coattails of my success.

Sometimes I'll be in a high-stakes situation and I'll be nervous and not sure what to say to the person I'm speaking to.

I might be asking for a salary or selling a company (or conducting any kind of sale at all), asking someone out on a date or talking to a friend who wants to apologize for something but I'm not sure if the relationship is worth continuing, or even talking to my children when they do something I don't approve of. So I outsource my decision to the person who is the decision-maker. It's a form of skipping the line that has worked for me every time to get even more than I had hoped for.

For example, someone approaches you with an offer to buy your company: "Well, we'd like to buy your company. How much do you want?"

You reply, "I have been so focused on building this to be the best company, I don't even know what the value of the company is. And I can see this growing ten times with a partner like your company. But you're like the grandmaster at this. You do deals like this all the time. I'm like an amateur." And you ask, "What advice would you give me in terms of how I value this?"

It may seem like you're giving the other side too much power, but it's the reverse. You're putting them on your side. You're in the same tribe and you are fully acknowledging their status in that tribe. By asking for advice you acknowledge their superiority in this decision.

When I ask for advice from a potential boss or even my children (and children often feel powerless), it acknowledges not only that they have more say in their situations than they thought but also that I think highly of them. Highly enough to trust them beyond the point where it is rational for me. Why would I ask a potential boss for advice on my salary if he just asked me flat out what I want my salary to be? Some might think I'm leaving the door open for him to screw me over. I'm also saying he's the "expert" at these things and that I trust him. All of these are further giving him a feeling of status over me.

I've just given status and trust to the other side. He's not going to risk losing it. He's primed to help me. He might not offer me twice what he was willing to pay, but I wasn't going to get that anyway even if I had asked for it. And then it would have been *me* who would've lost status.

And in these situations it's often very unclear what the correct solution is. I have less information than the other person. So no matter what he answers, it's information and information is power. I could've said, "Well, I was thinking of [ridiculously high number], but [insert advice technique here]."

That's called "anchoring bias." People will work off the number you anchor them with. It's been proven that if you are being asked what salary you should have and you say something, even as a joke, like, "Well, I was thinking of five million a year," and then you laugh, that tends to produce a higher salary.

But I don't like pulling that trick. That's just me. I'm uncomfortable, and if the boss senses I am doing that, it might backfire.

But the advice technique has never failed me. Mostly because I sincerely mean it. I'm terrified when a buyer asks me what I think my company or product is worth. I really want to know what he or she thinks.

So I ask for their advice. Give respect and acknowledge the other person's status. Serotonin will spike up in that person's brain. They will be happy, aggressive, and more willing to take risks. Like taking the risk of buying your company, hiring you, going out on a date with you, or a kid realizing she has more control over her destiny than she thought.

Remember that everyone has an agenda. But their primary agenda is to boost their self-worth and maintain their place in line (the hierarchy). When you interact with others, never try to boost your own self-worth. Always help people increase their own significance and their own self-worth. Do this sincerely and you have an ally for life.

Give them the power to help you.

They will.

SIX-MINUTE NETWORKING

To share your ideas, you have to have a network of people to share them with.

Jordan Harbinger had to restart his podcast. In 2018, he started *The Jordan Harbinger Show* with no listeners, after he and his partners at his prior show, *The Art of Charm*, decided to go their separate ways. Just eighteen months later he was getting millions of downloads a month. There's 800,000 podcasts out there.

"How did you rebuild and even go beyond so fast?" I asked him.

"I have this course called '6 Minute Networking,'" he said. "I wanted to call it '5 Minute Networking,' but that was already taken."

"Tell me what it is. And if you tell me, can I write about it?"

"Sure," he said, "but can you mention the name of my podcast when you write about it?"

"Of course. *The Jordan Harbinger Show.*"

OK, here it is: Every day at 1:00 p.m. EST (early for the West Coast, right when the East Coast is coming back from lunch, and not too late for Europe to see), do the following:

a. Scroll through your texts as far down as you can go. Find four people you haven't texted in a while.
b. Text them. Texts have a 90 percent open rate and emails only have about an 8 percent open rate.
c. Don't ask for anything. Just say, "I just saw XYZ and it reminded me of that project ABC you were working on. It gave me an idea you should do JKL. In any case, hope all is well. Talk to you soon."
d. Every day.

The idea, he said, is that you don't want anything from these people at all. You just want to be top of mind. At the end of the month, you'll have about another hundred people you are top of mind for.

The key, Jordan told me, "is to dig the well before you're thirsty."

So many things have happened to me since I adopted this practice.

Months later someone might ask one of the people you texted, "Do you know anyone who can speak at our executives retreat for a fee?" and because you are top of mind they might say, "James Altucher!"

Or you might get a consulting opportunity. Or maybe they know someone who would be an excellent guest on your podcast. It keeps you in contact.

I've done a version of this but not as systematically as Jordan. My previous technique was this: About once a week I'd go through my emails from seven years ago. If someone had written, "Hey, can we jump on a call for a few minutes?" and I never responded seven years ago, I might respond, "OK, how about Tuesday?" as if no time had passed at all. Rather than being annoyed, people were always surprised: "Does it always take you seven years to respond? Talk to you Tuesday!" The longest I ever took to hit Reply was twelve years. I hadn't spoken to the person in all of those twelve years. He had agreed to have lunch with me in 2002. In 2014, one week after I finally hit Reply after the twelve-year delay, he was on my podcast.

"Permission networking" is another practice Jordan explains in his course. It's one I've used for a long time too. Most people think their "network" is defined by their list of strong connections—the list of people they feel comfortable picking up a phone and calling.

So if you know 100 people, your network is worth 100. But this is not how to define the value of a network. There is the Facebook Rule of Networking: The value of your network is not the list of 100 people you know. The value of your network is all the connections between those 100 people you know.

So if your list is 100 people who don't know each other, then the value is 100. But if person A from your list and person B from your list also know each other—because you introduced them—then the value of your network is 101. The value goes up fast as you start introducing people to each other. Why? Because if you know 100 people, then there are 10,000 possible ways they can connect with each other (100 × 100).

My friend Lewis Howes built his business that way. He was living on his sister's couch, depressed over an injury that crushed his dream of being a professional athlete. He wanted to make connections, so he started connecting with people on LinkedIn. He would talk to his LinkedIn connections: So-and-so needed a lawyer. Lewis would make the introduction. So-and-so needed a programmer. He'd make the introduction. Then he started throwing parties where people would wear name tags that included their names and one thing they needed. His 100 connections quickly became worth 10,000 as everyone in his network met everyone else. He started selling courses on how to use LinkedIn for networking. His courses netted millions of dollars and his business began.

That's the power of networking, but to do it well, so that people really do help you and want to stay connected to you, you have to include one other element: permission.

The other day, the mayor of a certain city called me and said he wondered if I could introduce him to podcasts.

"Sure," I said.

So I called up several podcasts and said, "Is it OK if I introduce you to [famous mayor] for your podcast?"

I always get permission.

I hate when someone writes me an email and says, "James, meet Mr. X. I've cc'd him on this email. Moving myself to bcc, so you guys can take it from here!" Thanks but no thanks! You just gave me a homework assignment. I don't need more homework. You should have asked for permission first.

So I called people and said, "Do you want Mayor X?"

And they said, "Yes."

And I called the mayor and said, "Do you want to go on XYZ podcast?"

If he said yes, I'd make the introduction. I got permission on both sides. Now nobody resents the extra work I gave them. In fact, now I'm doing them both a favor. And I don't ask for *anything* in return. Being the source is enough.

And now my network's worth just went up. Do that every day and by the end of the year your network will be worth exponentially more than a year ago. Every day is the key. Just do one introduction. Don't make it hard for yourself.

When I have this book come out, I haven't asked for anything in my network. I've only delivered value. But now, because I've spent years prior delivering value in any way I can, I can ask, "Hey, I have a book coming out. Can you help me?" And people will say yes.

The reason this is called "six-minute networking" is that often things we think of as traditional networking—going to events or conferences, going to trade shows—are time-consuming and useless.

Along with the networking technique described on the previous pages, you also have to eliminate the time wasters that drag people down. Here are two ways to do that:

1. Never go to a "general" networking event. Unless it's for a specific topic or purpose, you will gain nothing except a fistful of useless business cards.

2. Create software to optimize your networking time.

Jordan told me, "I used Contactually to keep track of who I email and what commitments I make during email. I might say to someone via email, 'I'll get back to you in a month.' People appreciate consistency if one month later you get back to them. Else I forget."

Good! I always forget. I started doing this.

But what if you want to get in touch with someone who seems unreachable? Running a podcast, I'm always trying to get in touch with the unreachable.

"No problem," Jordan told me. "But the key is getting in touch with the tier right below the person. Celebrities usually have a wall of people blocking them from access by the outside world. Make those gatekeepers your network.

"But you can't just *show up.* They won't know you. You have to look at their social media, find something to bond on, and start with that. If someone is a big chess player, you can send a note and bond on that first."

And there it is, six minutes a day and it doesn't matter how much of an introvert or bad networker you are, your network will go up 100× in value over the course of the next year.

I've been a bad networker for thirty years. But the best time to start something is thirty years ago or today.

INVERT!

I never disagree with people. What for? If I believe in X and they believe in the opposite of X, what are the odds that I'm going to change their mind?

And if I change their mind, who cares? Will it change the world? Will they come to my funeral when I die?

But it's important to not get stuck in an opinion ghetto.

The "invert! technique" will not only help you deal with people you disagree with but allow you to experiment right in the middle of a conversation with someone who you disagree with.

Social media used to be called "social networks." You would connect with friends through a network and it was this brand-new way of keeping in touch. I loved it!

I suddenly refriended all the different archaeological layers of my life: my elementary school friends, high school friends, college friends, business friends, media friends, and so on.

But now, social networking has been replaced by "social media." The various social networks use their algorithms to figure out who agrees with you and they only show you those people's opinions on your "feed" (like we are animals feeding out of some information trough until we are bloated and sick).

The best way to get smarter is to find people of differing opinions and listen to them.

I am pro-choice. I listen to people who are pro-life.

I am anti-war. I listen to people who are pro-war.

I don't want my kids to go to college. I listen to people whose college experience is the best thing that ever happened to them.

Sometimes my mind changes. Sometimes people end up not liking me. This stresses me out.

But the best thing to do is not just listen to them but invert: seek out the opposite of what you believe to be true.

I don't let myself disagree with someone until I can argue for their position even *better* than they can. I have to know more, and I have to be willing to battle each of my original arguments.

In doing so, you become more well-rounded, more educated about how millions of people might think, and you feel less inclined to be angry or, worst of all, smug toward someone who doesn't agree with you. We're only humans for a short time. Why waste any of that time arguing with someone who has a different opinion than you about metal straws?

THE GOOGLE TECHNIQUE

When I started my first job, everyone warned me, "Bruce will steal credit for everything you do. Be careful." My friends were being kind to me. Credit, they thought, was something you hold on to like a precious gift and don't let anyone take from you.

But I wanted my boss to have credit. In part because the better he looked, the more likely I was to keep my job. I was terrified of being fired.

I gave Bruce credit for everything I did. I would tell everyone: This was Bruce's idea. Or Bruce let me do this. Or thank God I have a boss like Bruce. Bruce got promoted. And promoted and promoted. And he let me do more and more of what I wanted to do without saying anything. Because it always made him look good.

So eventually I started a company on the side. And then I hired my own company to do some of the work I was assigned to do.

Nobody cared. Because now I was enormously productive. And my boss got all the credit. And his boss. And his boss.

And then I quit. And then I went to my company full time.

Now what?

I made my clients look good.

Their job was to make great websites for their companies. I would make great websites for their companies. In meetings I would give them full credit for coming up with design ideas, functionality, business models, etc.

They looked good. They got promoted. They got hired at other companies. Who would they then hire to do their work? My company.

One time some of my employees wanted to quit to start their own company and even take some of our clients. My partners were furious! I said, "No problem." And I gave them advice. I made them look good. When I needed help twenty years later with something critical, they were the first to help me out. Not my old partners, but the employees who "betrayed" us. Be the credit card: give everyone the credit they deserve. Then they keep coming back to the source.

Careers are a marathon, not a sprint.

So what does this technique have to do with Google? Well, Google doesn't know anything about motorcycles. But if I go to Google and I ask, "Can you please tell me all about motorcycles?" it'll say, "Listen, we don't know anything about motorcycles, but we've done a lot of research and here are the ten best websites where you can learn about motorcycles."

It'll also say, "And by the way, these three websites over here might be good, but just so you know, they are paying us."

Google makes the best motorcycle sites look good. Google measures its success by how *quickly* its users *leave* Google.com. And now when I need to learn about the "best phones," what site do I go to? Not a phone site. I go to Google.

Some websites spend years trying to do SEO (search engine optimization) so they always appear near the top of Google's rankings. But Google is aware of this and is constantly changing and improving its algorithm so that it consistently ranks the highest quality websites near the top.

People always go back to the source. I realized when I was always making people look good, I was the source. They would come back to me. Whenever I needed a new job or a career, whenever I needed a favor, whenever I was in despair and thought I was lost, whenever I needed a hand to pick me up and get off the floor, I always found help from the people who at some point or other I made look good.

Every day find someone to help. Find someone to give credit to. Find someone for whom you can selflessly figure out how to make their lives easier. Need no credit ever and everyone will give you credit forever.

THE ATTENTION DIET

I was talking to Mark Manson, author of *The Subtle Art of Not Giving a F*ck*, which has sold eight million copies. It's a great book and he has a sharp writing style. He mentioned to me the concept of going on an "attention diet."

Here's my particular attention diet:

- I never watch the news.
- I never read a newspaper or a magazine.
- I never hit Home on Facebook.
- I never go to the Twitter home page.
- I get my news from books.
- I don't talk about North Korea or Trump or sports or what someone said when and to whom and why.
- If someone says, "Can you believe what is happening?" I always say, "Yes," and then I don't listen after that.
- If someone wants to pitch me an idea, I ignore it.
- If someone wants to meet me for coffee because "I'm sure you'd enjoy it," I ignore it.
- If someone gives me advice about finance, comedy, writing, economics, I ignore it.
- If someone disagrees with me, I ignore it *unless* I know them *and* it's face-to-face. Only 10 percent of communication is verbal.

"BUT WAIT . . . WON'T YOU BE UNINFORMED?"

No. I'll never be uninformed. If something is very important, life-changing important, friends will eventually ask me, "Did you hear . . . ?" and then I can look up original sources instead of the interpretations of whatever news source is reporting. This is going to be a very rare event. Very few news events survive in the public consciousness for more than a day.

If you read the highest quality history, philosophy, science, etc. books, then you understand the forces that shape the world, you can communicate it, and you can see the real facts that are shaping up over time.

You also learn how to live life better because you borrow the best features from the best authors.

If I live a better life, then it will uplift the people around me, who will uplift the people around them, and so on.

One stone dropping in the middle of the ocean sends waves to every shore.

"BUT WAIT . . . SHOULDN'T YOU BE AWARE OF WHAT'S HAPPENING IN YOUR OWN COUNTRY SO YOU CAN CREATE IMPACT?"

Instead of doing that, I can help the five or six homeless people who live within a block of me.

I can find senior citizens who are lonely and sit with them.

I can read to a blind person.

I can make people laugh.

Having impact on the things immediately around me is the best way to contribute value and alleviate suffering.

"BUT WAIT . . . WHY WOULD YOU IGNORE PEOPLE'S IDEAS? DON'T YOU ENCOURAGE PEOPLE TO HAVE IDEAS?"

Yes. I try to write down ten ideas every day. I've been doing this since 2002.

And I share those ideas when I need to. If I have ten ideas for McDonald's, I'll find some way to share them with someone at McDonald's.

Will they be good ideas? Probably not.

Which is why, usually, nobody should listen to my ideas. I've been practicing coming up with good ideas for eighteen years. So I'd rather work on my own creativity than listen to someone else's probably bad idea. Unless it's written in a book by an author either I enjoy or who has been heavily recommended to me.

THE "YES, AND . . ." TECHNIQUE

I wrote a book called *The Power of No.*

But now I'm about to tell you to say yes.

If someone presents an idea, the key is to say, "Yes, and . . ." Help them explore their idea. Help them be creative about their idea. "Yes, and . . ." is the first rule of good improv for a reason. It allows others to create something new.

The reason I bring this up is this: to get to the top, to skip the line, involves communicating with people all over the hierarchy. Often, to get your perspective across, you have to be able to critique other existing perspectives. People get defensive when you do this. Some people like to give destructive criticism. They like to fight, or they like feeling status over others (although this sort of status is very fleeting and damaging).

It's important to be able to use "Yes, and . . ." to give constructive criticism. Your criticism becomes win-win. It works like this:

- List what's good.
- Offer how you would improve upon the idea.
- Restate the core idea, its intention, and its purpose.

- Be open to the fact that you might be wrong. *Always, always* you might be wrong.
- Don't listen to destructive criticism or give it.

HOW TO HANDLE REJECTION

Imagine you decide to plagiarize one of the most successful books ever. You take a book that won a National Book Award and you retype it from scratch and pretend it's yours. You submit it to fourteen publishers. You put a fake name on it. One hundred percent of the publishers send back rejection letters. Two things strike you:

1. NONE of the publishers realized they rejected a National Book Award winner.

2. ALL of them thought the book was horrible—a book that had won the highest award.

This happened.

A freelance writer named Chuck Ross was curious. He took the book *Steps* by Jerzy Kosinski, which had won the National Book Award for Fiction in 1969, and decided to have some fun. He rewrote the entire book and then submitted it to publishers under a fake name. Not only did every publisher reject it, but even Random House, the publisher that actually published *Steps*, rejected it with a form letter. Kosinski's book had been compared to "Kafka at his best." It's a short, brutal book. One of my favorites. I highly recommend it.

Does this mean most people are idiots? Maybe.

It also means:

- Most people who have an opinion are probably wrong.
- If people don't know who you are, they are more likely to reject you.
- Nobody wakes up and says, "Today is the day I make some unknown person a superstar!"
- Most people don't care about their jobs. Which is fine. But don't rely on them for your success.
- Even successful people don't want you to skip the line. I always hear, "You have to pay your dues." This is BS.
- You have to take control of your own career and opportunities. You have to experiment constantly. You have to write down ten ideas a day to exercise your idea muscle. Nobody will come up with ideas for you. YOU have to come up with your ideas.
- You have a first book? Self-publish it. You have an indie movie? Upload it on Amazon. You have an idea for a radio show? Do a podcast.
- You have an app you want to build? Don't raise money. Save money and build it and get customers. Or simply make an ad about it before you even build the app and see if anyone clicks (an experiment to see if people are interested in your idea).
- You want to be a movie star? Write your own script (e.g., what Sylvester Stallone did with *Rocky*) or shoot your own movie.

It's a catch-22 because in order to be good, you have to be unique. But in order to be unique, nobody can know you. And nobody does favors for the unknown. You have to find the room nobody else is in and then invite everybody to join you. This is skipping the line.

I decided to try my own light experiment. I wanted to pull a Chuck Ross and see if I could have better luck in our new self-published world.

I took *Fifty Shades of Grey* and hired someone in India to take a the-saurus and change every word in the book. For instance, "She hurried to her tests" became "Brenda rushed to get to the exams on time."

I used a fake name, changed the title, made a book cover, and up-loaded it to Amazon. It's now a published book. It's EXACTLY *Fifty Shades of Grey* but with every single word changed, sentence by sen-tence. Maybe . . . just maybe . . . I was hoping it would also sell a lot of copies. It sold about eighty copies. It's a piece of s***. But it cost me about $200 in total and two hours of my time. It was an experiment.

Why did *Fifty Shades of Grey* sell so well? What did E L James do? Doing my failed experiment forced me to learn:

> - She had a platform. She probably had about a million people fol-lowing her *Twilight* fan fiction on various websites.
> - *Fifty Shades of Grey* came out around the same time the Kindle was getting popular. So people could read her soft-core porn in public without anyone seeing what they were reading, thus avoid-ing the stigma.
> - It was unique.

She had a platform. And technology and timing were just right. But she would never have known that unless she had experimented, built a platform, wrote her own book without "permission," and self-published.

Good for her.

This is not about self-publishing. This is not about how people are stupid (well, it is a little).

This is about not waiting for permission.

This is about doing experiments with everything you care about.

And from every experiment you will learn. There's no other way to learn.

A billion people are standing in the way of what you want to do.

Stupid people, mean people, people who hate you, people who don't want you to get ahead. People who will even sabotage you.

People who are frustrated in their own lives, dealing with their own problems—sad, anxious, fearful.

Experiment with how to get around them. Every day. It's not their fault. But that doesn't matter. You have to go around them.

You have to experiment every single day.

CHAPTER 14

THE 50/1 RULE (OR HOW TO BE INFINITELY PRODUCTIVE)

I've had one corporate job in my life. People got to work around 10:00 a.m. Around 11:30 they'd take a cigarette break downstairs. Around noon they went to lunch. Around 3:30 another cigarette break. By 4:50 people would start leaving. And when they weren't hard at work in their cubicles, they attended useless meetings, socialized at the water fountain, flattered the boss, and so on. I guesstimated that people worked on average about two to three hours a day.

OK, I don't want to imply that this is everybody, so maybe I should use the all-powerful Google to help me here. One second . . .

OK, from Google: the average worker is "productive" 2 hours 53 minutes a day. Google sent me over to *Inc.* magazine. Here's what *Inc.* had to say about what unproductive things people do during the day:

1. Read news websites—1 hour 5 minutes

2. Check social media—44 minutes

3. Discuss non-work-related things with coworkers—6 minutes

4. Search for new jobs—26 minutes

5. Take smoke breaks—23 minutes

6. Make calls to partners or friends—18 minutes

7. Make hot drinks—17 minutes

8. Text or instant message—14 minutes

9. Eat snacks—8 minutes

10. Make food in office—7 minutes

Makes sense. But the question is, in those 2 hours 53 minutes that people are productive, what are they doing? Does productive time include official meetings where nothing gets done? (And I like how the average worker is searching for a new job twenty-six minutes a day.)

When you make a salary, they are paying you just enough to do a job you don't like. I wouldn't shovel shit if you paid me $100,000 a year. But I can guarantee you I'd do it for at least a year if you paid me $10,000,000 a year.

But if you can explore what you love and get paid for it, then it's bliss. Warren Buffett always says, "I skip to work every day." And his official salary is only $100,000. (OK, that's because he doesn't want to pay taxes and he already has $72 billion, but still.)

This doesn't mean you shouldn't work hard. Nor does it mean you can take shortcuts and find success at work, or even at home. Because here's the thing about work: you don't really make money from the value you create.

If the work I do results in an extra $1 in value for the company, how much of that do I get to take home? Well, the shareholders take a cut. And the CEO takes a chunk. And my boss and her boss and his boss and her boss take a cut. And they all take bigger cuts than me. So maybe out of $1 in value that I create I get to keep 1 cent. Maybe much less.

This is not to say that you should sit around and do nothing. But now I want to show you a technique that will optimize the time you work to make it as effective as possible so then you can use all the remaining time for finding your obsessions, pursuing them, learning them, and mastering them.

I used to lock myself in the conference room for an hour or so a day—not answering when people knocked to get in—while I called clients for my side business making websites for other companies. I'd really sweat it out when people were banging on the door. I'm sweating now thinking about it. And I'm writing this during the Covid-19 lockdown, so I haven't changed clothes in a couple of days, and now I'm sweating and it's not pleasant. But I remember.

It took me eighteen months to go from HBO, my full-time job where I was making $42,500 a year (and that was after a raise), to my "side gig" building websites, where I was CEO, had twenty employees, and was making more than my full-time job.

Back then, I was afraid to take risks. And I wish Tim Ferriss's *4-Hour Workweek* existed when I worked at HBO, but it didn't. Because then I would have learned the 80/20 Rule and how it changes productivity. And then I would've added a twist that I haven't seen anyone ever bring up. The 80/20 Rule is the idea that 20 percent of the time you spend on a project creates 80 percent of the value. It works in every area of life. It's practically like a law in physics. (Actually, it's called the Pareto principle. Look it up.) If you have a garden and plant seeds, then 20 percent of the seeds will create 80 percent of the flowers.

If you have one hundred employees, then twenty of your employees will generate 80 percent of your revenue.

If you own a business, 20 percent of your customers will generate 80 percent of your revenue.

If you are Amazon.com, 20 percent of the books being sold in your enormous online bookstore will generate 80 percent of your book sales.

Former *Wired* editor Chris Anderson coined the phrase "the long tail" to describe how, in our new digital world, everyone has the chance to monetize a little. The long tail is actually the opposite of the 80/20 Rule, but it's interesting to think about. Yes, 20 percent of the authors in the world generate 80 percent of the book sales in the world—authors like J. K. Rowling, John Grisham, etc. But what Chris Anderson noticed was that because every book is available online now, almost every author (the other 80 percent of the authors that are not at the top) participates in that final 20 percent of book sales. Most authors might only sell one or two books, but his point is that there is a short tail (those few at the top generating the most sales) and then there is a very long tail of people who still generate some sales. His point implied that if you were an aggregator (like Amazon) of all the books, you'd generate a lot of money from the long tail. This is another way of making use of the knowledge of the 80/20 Rule.

Tim Ferriss's point is this: you don't need to work 100 percent of the time to create 100 percent of the value if you know that just 20 percent of your time can create almost as much value (specifically: 80 percent). This means, if you are a business, for instance, that you have to be fine with a reduction in revenue. If your business previously made

$1 million but took up 100 percent of your time, then now you have to be fine making $800,000 (80 percent of the original revenue) but using only 20 percent of your time.

Now the question (and the benefit) is: What do you do the other 80 percent of the time? Do you do the unproductive activities listed on pages 169–170 or do you develop new skills, increase your networking (see the "Six-Minute Networking" section in chapter 13: "Microskills Everyone Should Learn"), and start to cultivate new sources of income?

According to the IRS, the average multimillionaire has seven sources of income. A job is only one source of income. So if you use up 100 percent of your time to get the maximum 100 percent of revenue from one job, then you will make less than someone who efficiently does the *right* 20 percent three times a day on three different activities to generate 240 percent (80 percent × 3) of their normal revenue; plus they'll have an additional 40 percent of time leftover per week.

How do you find the right 20 percent? This is the hard part, and there's no clear answer.

- You can eliminate all the unproductive activities mentioned on pages 169–170, and that will help you wipe out about 60–70 percent of unproductive time.
- You can eliminate or cut short meetings, since they are rarely productive.
- You can have a list of top priorities that you know *need* to get done and start trimming the fat off and then just focus on those activities.
- You can acknowledge that you don't need to generate 100 percent of the output you normally do—that 80 percent is fine and achieved with much less stress.

> • You can keep a diary of all your activities for a few weeks and then measure how productive each activity was. How much in revenue did it generate, for instance? By measuring your activities, you can help whittle down that 100 percent of work to the most efficient 20 percent.

Tim Ferriss explains that he was a perfectionist at school and was very unhappy if he got less than an A or A+ on a test. But to get that extra 20 percent on his test scores he'd have to work many more hours. Instead, if he was satisfied with a steady B he could reduce his studying by 80 percent and spend time learning other skills.

You have to be fine with that.

But we're going to take that 20 percent down to 1 percent in a second using a twist of the 80/20 Rule.

◆ ◆ ◆

One time I was in a taxi and I started talking to the driver. He had an accent and said he was from Turkey. Somehow it came up that he played chess.

"Oh!" I said. "I play chess also." I figured he knew the rules and was a casual player and we could chat about it. In the U.S. ranking system, I am ranked a "master," and just obtaining that title has given me many benefits in life. When people hear "chess master," they incorrectly think "smart." Just because this has been on my résumé most of my life, I've gotten into college and graduate school, I've gotten job offers, and I've even raised money simply because people think being a chess master means I'm smart. Bad assumption!

I asked the cab driver if he ever played in tournaments.

"Yes, I was the national champion of Turkey."

"What!?"

"Yes. I am an international master."

Which meant he was quite a bit stronger than me. He told me it took him five extra years of studying and playing in tournaments constantly to go from the rank of master to international master. In other words, I put in 20 percent of the work he did, but I was "only" a master and he was a top-ranking international master. But if I had put in those five extra years of work, what would it have done for me? People who hired me, or invested with me, or worked with me on various opportunities would not have cared or even known the difference if I was a master or an international master. Most people would just think it was the same thing. And even to the average chess player, it is the same thing. The average player wouldn't be able to tell the difference between our styles of play, although I would be able to (he would beat me at least two out of three times). This is a case where I had my priorities straight, stopped playing in tournaments when I hit that first goal (master), and used that title to obtain the benefits that society gives to people who excel in activities considered "smart."

You have to take a step back and see which activities, and for how long, can give you the most gain in the goals you want to achieve.

Now . . . the twist.

The 80/20 Rule applies to itself.

If you 80/20 the 80/20 Rule, you get the 64/4 Rule. Four percent of the seeds planted in the garden get you 64 percent of the value.

(80 percent × 80 percent = 64 percent and 20 percent × 20 percent = 4 percent.)

Gardeners can confirm this turns out to be true.

Four percent of your work gives you 64 percent of the value you create.

Four percent of your investments in life will give you 64 percent of your overall investment earnings.

And so on.

Do it one more time.

Let's apply the 80/20 Rule to the 64/4 Rule.

It turns out that roughly 1 percent of the value will give you 50 percent of the value. (Technically, 0.8 percent of the work will give you about 51.2 percent of the value.)

How can you find the right 1 percent of activities so that you generate 50 percent of the value you are currently generating while using 100 percent of your time?

Imagine you're an employer and you have one hundred employees.

According to the 50/1 Rule, one of your employees is generating approximately 50 percent of the value of your company.

Who is that one? Or who are the four that are generating 64 percent? Or who are the twenty that are generating 80 percent of your revenue?

Measure what matters.

- Define what "value" is. Is it revenue? Is it profit? Is it "closing new sales"?
- Start measuring. Which twenty people generated 80 percent of new sales this past month (for instance)? Which four of those twenty generated 80 percent of that 80 percent? And which one of those was the best?

For a month, write down on a calendar what you do all day, even the most obscure items, like: "Went to bathroom from 10:03 to 10:05." Many people, when looking back at their day, don't remember or even realize how much of their time they spend on unproductive things.

Then, at the end of the month, with all this data, and with you determining what priorities you consider important, figure out the 1 percent of time when you created the most output. Now, if you are OK with being half as productive but using only 1 percent of the prior amount of time you would have spent on an activity, you can now adjust your schedule to do *just* that 1 percent. That doesn't mean you binge-watch Netflix the other 99 percent. Although it could. Sometimes that's not such a bad idea. Downtime and rejuvenation time are important for the brain, for creativity, and for stress relief.

But now you can also decide what other activities you want to explore. You've just freed up almost all of your time. Yes, you might be making half of what you were before, but life is good and you have time to pursue other interests, other moneymaking activities, or other creative activities that could turn into bigger opportunities.

Example: When I created Stockpickr, a social networking site for people interested in investing, it had many features. It had the stock portfolios of famous investors so people could maybe study the stock picks of investing giants like Warren Buffett, Carl Icahn, etc. The site could connect users and allow them to send messages to each other. It also had message boards where people could start a thread like "Google Is the Best Stock!" and everyone could discuss. Users could also enter their own portfolios and an algorithm would match their portfolios to other similar portfolios so they could connect with like-minded people and perhaps discuss their investments. Finally, it had a page that listed the results of various stock screens, like "What Stocks Fell the Most Yesterday" or "What Stocks Do the Best in May."

I was very proud of all the features. When I studied the traffic, though, I saw that most of the pageviews were in the message boards. Hardly any traffic was going through portfolios. Twenty percent of my effort in the site was devoted to participating in the message boards, and that was creating at least 80 percent of the traffic. And then I looked further. Most of the traffic on the message boards was in message threads that started with a question, like "What stocks are undervalued right now?" or "What stocks have the highest dividends?"

It turned out that 4 percent of the site (message boards that started with a question) was generating at least 60 percent of the traffic. So I tried something new, and it took me about a day to program. I created a section of the site that was *just* for questions and answers. Ask any question and other users could answer. The very same day that I launched the Q and A portion of the site, the site doubled in pageviews. So by studying which 20 percent was producing the most value, I was able to focus on improving that area in order to generate more traffic. More traffic led to more ads on the site, which led to more revenue.

Then I noticed something else. One person, a well-known investor, was answering a lot of the questions that people asked on the Q and A page. In fact, his answers seemed to be generating about 50 percent of the pageviews on the entire site. He was my 1 percent! So I found other well-known investors and asked them to answer questions on the site. Traffic to the site again doubled.

By using the 50/1 Rule (derived from the 80/20 Rule) and defining how I measured success (in this case, pageviews), I was able to improve the business and also free up time. Instead of updating my stock screens every day, I only did it once a week. It didn't really change the business at all. And instead of updating all the stock portfolios of the superstar investors, I would only update a handful of them. I realized the site was mostly a Q and A site about investing. In this way I was able to quickly create enough pageviews, revenue, and value for the business that I was able to sell it only a few months after I launched it.

Another friend of mine started a blog. She would blog about her day, about her family, about her husband, etc. She never thought to look at her analytics to see which posts were doing better than others. Once she did, she realized that her posts with parenting tips (about 20 percent of the posts) were generating most of her pageviews. So she started doing more posts with parenting tips and her pageviews went up. When she dug deeper, her posts with tips about her techniques for teaching and disciplining her kids under the age of five were getting significantly more pageviews than her posts about her teenage kids. So she started doing more of those. Because her site started getting so many pageviews, she began to sell advertising, which allowed her to quit her job. From what started as a hobby for her, incorporating the 80/20 Rule . . . on top of the 80/20 Rule . . . on top of the 80/20 Rule ultimately changed her life.

This rule doesn't only apply to your workdays; it can be useful in every aspect of your life.

In 2012, I was so busy all the time, I hated my life. I was writing too many blog posts. I was trying to go on various news shows so that I would remain (in my demented mind) "relevant." I was trying too hard to find moneymaking opportunities everywhere and ended up spending too much time going down very deep rabbit holes but with no results. Or I would travel for business meetings that would take me out of my routine for two or three days and usually have no results. I was on the board of directors of several companies and that was a magnificent waste of time. Nobody wanted to listen to my guidance until the companies were on the verge of bankruptcy, and by then there was no hope.

So I quit all the boards I was on. I stopped advising companies. I stopped going on news shows (huge waste of time and energy for three minutes of glory). I even stopped starting companies. I realized that half the money I made in the prior few years was from passive investments in existing companies. My number one rule in investing: always invest alongside people smarter than me. My advice should never be needed. I don't need to have any board seats. I just need to stand on the shoulders of the greats.

For instance, in 2006, I was on CNBC and everyone was laughing at me. I had just written in an article for the *Financial Times* that Facebook, which had just been offered $1 billion by Microsoft, was right to turn that offer down because I felt they would one day be worth more than $100 billion. One hundred times as much. Everyone said I was a fool. Still, I felt like Facebook was a "miniature and organized internet"—that's how I put it. I wanted to invest in the company but didn't know how. But I did know how I had monetized the trend of the internet ten years earlier. I had started a web development agency helping big corporations use this new tool called the World Wide Web.

It was a perfect idea sex moment! Facebook + the old way I monetized the internet = a Facebook ad agency that would help corporations get onto the internet. I started looking for one, and in the summer of 2007 I found one being started by a friend of mine, Michael Lazerow. But I wouldn't invest unless people smarter than me were in the deal too. Well, it turns out Peter Thiel, the first outside investor in Facebook, would be investing alongside people like me at the exact same terms. I'm in! During the next few years, even when I wanted to give advice to the CEO, Michael, he barely ever returned my phone calls. I was useless. Exactly where I wanted to be. They never needed advice from me. In 2012, they sold to Salesforce.com for $800 million.

I spent even less than 1 percent of my time on that company, Buddy Media, between the years 2007 and 2012, but it accounted for about 50 percent of the money I made during those years. So I decided to eliminate everything else that I used to do to make money *except* for investing in private companies that I wouldn't have to advise. I would invest only if there were other investors smarter than me (not so difficult) putting their money into the same company at the same terms as me.

I stopped doing 99 percent of what I had been doing, a lot of which I hated doing anyway.

Now I had a lot of extra time. I was spending only about 1 percent of the time I used to spend on moneymaking activities. Maybe I would make less—fifty percent less—but with the time I was saving, I could start pursuing the activities I love and monetize those activities. I started doing this toward the end of 2012. I wrote my book *Choose Yourself!* and published it in June 2013. It became my bestselling book out of twenty books I've written. And at the end of 2013, I started my podcast, *The James Altucher Show*, which has since had almost 100 million downloads and has been a huge pleasure for me.

When I started the podcast, I asked myself: What kinds of guests generate the most downloads? At the start, about 80 percent of my guests were celebrities that I felt obligated to have on because they were celebrities. I felt people were more likely to download a show with a celebrity than with a noncelebrity. The other 20 percent of my guests were people who'd done something extraordinary or who had written a book on a subject that I was insanely curious about. *Those* were the episodes with the most downloads—because my curiosity showed, and the listeners appreciated it and were more likely to share those episodes with their friends.

This approach works in comedy too. I was watching a special by one of my favorite comedians. I was measuring all sorts of things: how many seconds between each time the audience laughed, how loud the laughs were, what types of jokes the comedian was doing, etc. He's a great comedian and every joke had been carefully honed over years of work, and he was funny throughout the hour of his special. But I noticed that whenever he did a voice, that is, when he acted out a character that sounded funny in his jokes, the laughter was louder and lasted longer. I don't know if it would make his act better to do more voices—maybe people would get tired of it—but I noticed that in my own comedy sets, I was never doing voices. So I started adding them in and I started experimenting onstage with more "act-outs," where instead of just telling a joke about various people I would act out the joke by playing the roles of those characters. You guessed it: more laughs.

The 50/1 Rule works. I don't make anywhere near as much money on podcasting as I do on investing in private companies (in fact, to this day, I make zero money on the podcast), but it's what I love doing and I don't mind that I potentially make 50 percent less overall than what I could be making if I spent all of my time on moneymaking activities. I hated going to board meetings even if it made me more money. I hated doing any sort of consulting even if it made me more money. And I love writing and doing podcasts. What else is life for than to make enough that you do well and also have plenty of time to do the things you love?

I found the right 1 percent that created 50 percent of my income, and it allowed me to pursue new ideas and new creative opportunities, read more books, spend more time with people I like, and binge-watch the entire series of *Lost* at least six times. No more consulting (blech!), no more board seats (ugh!), no more business travel (unless I have some vacation time baked in). And I make less! But there's more time to do what I love.

It doesn't always work out great. Some years I make nothing. Other years I make quite a bit. Some years I start to get nervous and wonder if I will ever make money again. But I have faith in this 50/1 Rule, and for the past nine years it's worked exactly as promised.

CHAPTER 15

TAKE TWO STEPS BACK

Joey Coleman wanted to work for the Secret Service, the White House, or the CIA, but he had no idea how to get a job with any of those places.

"I got to D.C. to begin law school and I called the Secret Service, but they had no law clerk program. But they did have a college intern program."

He applied to be a college intern, and the head of the internship program called him and she said, "There must be a mistake here. You might be overqualified for this. This is just an undergraduate intern program and you're in law school."

"That's right," Joey said. "And, listen, I'm happy to make copies, get people coffee, whatever the undergraduate interns do, but maybe there's a slight chance someone in the general counsel's office at the Secret Service would be interested in having a law student do some research."

Joey later told me, "I wanted to help the head of the intern program look good. If she shows up at the general counsel's office and says she has a free law clerk for everyone, then she is providing them what could be a service they very much need. And for free! Or, worst case, I'm just an overqualified intern, but I get to see how the Secret Service operates."

He got the position. And the office of the general counsel of the Secret Service was ecstatic to know they had an intern they could call on for legal research. Joey spent almost the entire summer working on issues critical to the Clinton administration during an election year. And, most important, he got "secret" security clearance. When he got back to law school for his second year, he called the White House. It turned out they did have a law clerk program, but it was mostly made up of elite-of-the-elite students from the top law schools—Harvard, Yale, Stanford—and they only accepted seven law school students out of tens of thousands who applied.

"I wasn't editor of my school's law review, for instance," Joey told me. "I didn't think I had any chance of getting to be one of the seven clerks.

"But," he continued, "they have an undergraduate intern program at the White House. So I apply. And the same thing happens. The head of the intern program calls me and says, 'I think you applied for the wrong program. This is for college students.'"

Joey said to her, "I know. I'm happy to be an intern and make copies, file things, get people coffee, and whatever else the undergraduate interns do. But, you can tell the legal counsel's office at the White House that you have a second-year law student in the intern program just in case they need, for free, an extra set of eyes doing legal research or preparing briefs. Turns out they needed it very much! This was during an election year, during Whitewater, so many things happening, that they were ecstatic to have me."

"And," he told the woman who ran the White House internship program, "I have 'secret' clearance and I know everyone in the White House needs 'top secret' clearance, so since I already have 'secret,' it will be easier to get me approved."

So he started working at the White House undergraduate intern program even though he was a second-year law student. He ended up spending most of the year doing legal research and preparing legal briefs right in the heart of the White House.

"After that, I wanted to work at the CIA during the summer program," Joey told me. "And it turns out they do have a law clerk program, but again it's very difficult to get into." He applied and noted that he had top secret clearance already. "It takes months to get top secret security clearance. It made it easy for the CIA to accept me rather than have to go through the time and expense of clearing me for that."

While at the CIA, he was offered a full-time job. "I was torn," he told me. "I thought about it for at least six months but ultimately decided to work for my dad at his law firm and be a criminal defense attorney." After a few years of that he went on to start a successful ad agency.

Fast-forward a decade. I met Joey in 2013 because we were both speaking at the same conference. At the end of the conference, the audience could vote for the speaker who provided the most value, and that speaker would win $30,000.

I gave a good talk. But it wasn't enough. Joey crushed it in a landslide.

"That was only my second time giving a talk," he told me. "But I told myself that if I win this speaking contest, I'm going to be a full-time professional speaker."

He won, and now he's one of the most successful corporate speakers in the country.

What was his secret? "Before the talk I called up Jayson Gaignard, host of the conference, and asked him for the names of everyone who would be in the audience.

"I knew from my time as a criminal defense attorney two things: When you call someone by their name it humanizes them. So a defense attorney will always use the client's name, while the prosecutor will try to dehumanize by referring to my clients as 'the defendant.' I also learned that, of course, a picture is worth a thousand words."

So in the middle of his talk, he weaved in the idea that it is important to "know your audience, know your customer," and he flashed a slide that had photos from everyone's Facebook pages. I remember that he had a photo of me holding up my newborn baby from 2002. It brought tears to my eyes.

Everyone voted for Joey. It wasn't even close. And he went from being a lawyer and ad agency founder to being a successful public speaker overnight.

When I told him the topic of the book I was working on, he shouted at me, "Every part of my career I owe to skipping the line!"

In his case, he skipped ahead by falling two steps behind his peers. He took internships designed for people with half his experience and education. Taking this kind of leap isn't just a practical matter—it's hard on the ego, it's hard on our natural-born instincts to stick with our tribe and maintain our status. But if you can take a leap backward, you will eventually be able to leapfrog past those who have been dutifully plodding along.

Joe Moglia was the CEO of Ameritrade for seven years. While he was there he increased the value of the company from a meager $700 million to $12 billion. He was one of the most skilled CEOs on Wall Street, creating value for the shareholders of Ameritrade and eventually selling the company to the Canadian bank Toronto-Dominion. The result of the merger was TD Ameritrade, of which he was CEO, and he could've continued at that role, creating immense wealth for himself.

Instead . . . he quit in March 2008. "I wasn't excited anymore," he told me. He realized the happiest time in his life was when he was coaching football.

He went back to his first love: sports. He had been an athlete as a kid. And after he got a master's degree in education, he'd been a football coach. For sixteen years he was a coach, finally ending that career in 1983 when he left his position as defensive coordinator for the Dartmouth College football team. Now he wanted to coach again. But he had been out of the industry for twenty-five years. "You can't do that!" is what he heard many times. Nobody would hire him, even though he had been a coach for sixteen years and then CEO of a multibillion-dollar company. Finally he went to see Bo Pelini, head football coach at the University of Nebraska, and offered to be his assistant. Pelini said, "Sure. Why not?"

Every day Moglia would go to practice and take notes. He would study the playbooks and attend the coaches' meetings. He would speak up at team meetings when he thought he had something to say. Otherwise, he just listened and learned.

In 2011, he became the head coach of the United Football League's Omaha Nighthawks, and then a year later he joined the Coastal Carolina University football team as head coach. In his first year they won the conference championship and he was named Big South Football Coach of the Year. In 2019, after successfully coaching for six seasons, he stepped down and retired, having fulfilled a dream he'd had since the 1960s of being a successful college coach. While at Coastal Carolina, he led the team to 56 wins and 22 losses, an incredible record.

If he had been obsessed with where he was in the hierarchy, he never would have retired from a job where he could have made billions of dollars to reduce his status to the level of "assistant." Not even "assistant coach."

Even a single thought where you are concerned about your own self-worth will block any chances of success in your passion. Always pursue making the others around you look as good as possible. In Moglia's case, he was dedicated to making coach Bo Pelini of Nebraska as successful as possible. Pelini returned the favor by mentoring the sixty-year-old successful bank CEO on what it takes to be a great coach.

Only then was he able to take three steps forward and fulfill his dream of becoming a successful college football head coach.

CHAPTER 16

WOBBLE WITHOUT FALLING DOWN

I almost ruined my career right at the beginning.

Back in 1992, two years before I actually started working at HBO, they offered me a different job. I wish I had taken it. They wanted me to work on this new field: "virtual reality." I never responded to them. I felt inadequate.

How come?

I didn't want to take a job in the "real world" until I felt people would like me. I had so little self-esteem that I thought the only way people would like me at a place like HBO was if I had published a novel. So I wrote and wrote and wrote. I wrote a novel called "The Book of Orpheus" (a corny, cliché title written by a twenty-four-year-old). It was a four-hundred-page novel about the person I wanted to be in my wildest dreams instead of a novel about the real me. Then, after forty-plus rejections of that novel—which took over a year to write—I wrote another novel. The title: "The Book of David" (I know). It was about the biblical David but from a very alternative point of view.

Forty-plus rejections.

I wrote another novel, "The Prostitute, The Porn Novelist, The

Romance Novelist, and Their Lovers" (a play on the movie *The Cook, the Thief, His Wife & Her Lover*).

Forty-plus rejections.

I wrote forty to fifty short stories. Thousands of rejections.

I wrote novellas. I read thousands of books and then criticisms of those books because I wanted to get better.

I was so afraid to show up to the real world empty-handed. Nobody would like me. Nobody would think I was special. I had such low self-esteem. I felt that if people didn't think I was special (people secretly whispering to each other, "Who is he?" "Him? He wrote a novel!"), then they would hate me or, worse, not pay attention to me. Women would spit on me. Everyone would laugh at my ideas.

By the time I was twenty-six years old, in 1994, I was starting to get afraid I'd never succeed as a writer, I was unhappy at my job, and I was unhappy in my relationship. I was so bad at difficult conversations that I decided the only way out of the relationship was to move to New York City. So I took the job at HBO even though I still hadn't met my goal of becoming a famous writer everyone loved and respected. Out of thousands and thousands of pages I'd written, I never published a single one.

It was hard to get that job in 1994, but a few months later I was in New York City for my first day. I was in a suit, settling down in my cubicle at the HBO building. For the first three months, I screwed up so badly they had to send me to remedial computer classes even though I had majored in computer science and went to grad school for it.

I was the worst employee. I was sure they were going to fire me every day.

I was afraid nobody would like me because I wasn't some "perfect" ideal of myself. I always wanted to stand out and be special, or else I would be "discovered" for the fraud that I was. But after a few months of trying to come up with ideas that would make me stand out, I finally figured it out. HBO at that time didn't have a website. They didn't have an intranet for their internal employees. Most of the employees didn't even know what the web was. So one weekend I stayed there for forty-eight straight hours. I created an intranet and installed a web browser (Mosaic, the first browser, created by a young student at the University of Illinois named Marc Andreessen) on about a hundred machines. When everyone got to the office on Monday morning, the excitement everyone had over this new tool completely changed my career.

They say "perfection is the enemy of progress," but there's a bit more to it. You have to be willing to wobble your way through to success. I was twenty-six and scared and unqualified for the job. Nothing was the way I wanted it to be. I wasn't a successful novelist that everyone would admire my first day at the job. I wasn't even that qualified for the job. In fact, I didn't really know anything.

I had to learn to wobble into a situation, to be OK with falling and getting back up, to be OK with not being perfect in advance.

❦ ❦ ❦

The Wright brothers ran a bicycle shop. People love to ride bicycles. The U.S. government was spending $2 million to get a plane in the air. The Wright brothers (from their tiny bike shop) were racing against the wealthy U.S. government to fly. Who would fly first?

The government was convinced that a plane had to fly straight or it would crash. No turbulence. Zero imperfections, or else it would fail. The Wright brothers thought this also. Until one day . . . they looked at a little kid learning to ride a bike. He jumped on the bike and took off. He wobbled for a few seconds, and every turn he wobbled again, but soon he was off and gone. He was riding a bike.

He wobbled!

They made a plane that wobbled. The plane flew. They made history. They beat out a government that was spending millions. They did it by focusing on progress rather than perfection.

"Progress" is skipping the line. "Perfection" means you're going to wait in line forever.

Don't be afraid to wobble.

It's difficult to not be afraid. In 1956, John F. Kennedy published a book, *Profiles in Courage*, about people in history who against public opinion and at the risk of losing the support of those who loved them stood up for what they felt was right. The book won a Pulitzer Prize. The fact that a book about eight people in history who had courage was important enough to win a Pulitzer Prize shows how rare it is to have courage. To stand up and be hated for your opinions and still press forward with compassion and insight, knowing that what you are doing is creating value: this is true courage.

Still, it's not so easy to be the person who stands up for his beliefs and doesn't care what people think. Everyone decides which masks to wear, which battles to fight. Nobody is fearless all the time.

But what if you can turn the fear into growth?

» I GET SCARED EVERY TIME I DO A PODCAST. I'm shy and I'm afraid I'll seem stupid and that the guest won't like me. I'm afraid they will yell at me. I'm afraid they will think I'm unprepared, or that the listeners will hate the show, or that I'm not doing a good enough job. Every guest intimidates me.

» I GET SCARED EVERY TIME I START A BUSINESS. What if I fail? What if people think I'm a loser? What if I go broke? What if I can't afford to raise my kids after I go broke? What if nobody will like me after I go broke?

» I GET SCARED EVERY TIME I DO STAND-UP COMEDY. I'm going on a stage like a clown in a room full of strangers. What if they don't laugh? What if they laugh *at* me instead of *with* me? What if they heckle me and hate me? Even worse: What if they are silent? What if the other comedians and the booker at the club see how bad I am when I bomb?

» I GET SCARED EVERY TIME I HIT PUBLISH ON AN ARTICLE. Or even worse, a book. What if it doesn't do well? What if people think I've lost my touch? (Did I ever even have a touch?) What if people think, "He's been telling the same stupid story for years"? What if people read it and hate me for it and start posting hate messages about me? What if friends stop talking to me because they disagree with me? What if I lose any skill or talent I've had and I have to spend the next forty years wishing that skill was back?

Every time I'm scared, I ask myself: Is this the opportunity I've been waiting for? Is this the chance to do something nobody has done before?

I don't start a business *unless* I'm afraid it will fail. If it were so easy, then how come someone hasn't done it already? I know I'm not that smart.

I don't give a talk or go on a stage *unless* I'm afraid I'm going to say something that's going to challenge people a bit too much. Because that's the only way they'll remember the talk. Because if I don't challenge the way they think, then they will never think about my talk.

I don't hit Publish on an article *unless* I'm afraid of what people will think of me. Then I know I am saying something new, something that is pushing a boundary both for the readers and for me.

Lean in to the fear to create growth. Fear is the catalyst. And growth is the reason you hit Publish. The reason you speak up. The reason you try something new. The reason you step out of line.

CHAPTER 17

EXIT THE LINE

Jonathan couldn't believe it. "They laid off everyone and no severance." The company he'd worked for went out of business. Laid everyone off in an email. Locked the doors. Didn't respond to calls and emails. The employees set up a GoFundMe to try to raise some extra cash. I shared the link. A few people donated.

"What are you going to do next?"

"I don't know," he said. "I was there for five years. I was excited about what I was doing. I didn't have a plan B."

❥ ❥ ❥

It's OK if you love your job. It's OK if you don't want to quit and be an entrepreneur.

You can be an "entreployee," using the skills of entrepreneurship, the skills described in this book, to be successful at your job.

But you still need a plan B. Forty years ago . . . even fifteen years ago . . . maybe not. But nothing is holy ground anymore. To borrow a phrase from Nassim Nicholas Taleb, investor and author, you need to be "antifragile."

"Fragile" is when you are fired and you crash and burn and get depressed and go broke.

"Resilient" is when you are fired but you have six months savings and you dress up in a suit and apply for new jobs and after four months you find one. It's a slightly lower salary and longer commute, but you'll survive and live to fight another day.

"Antifragile" is when you are hit hard and you recover even stronger than you were before. Have a plan B that makes you antifragile. Again, you don't want to get fired, but if it happens, you'll bounce back stronger than you were before.

Why? People used to get a job for the stability. My grandfather started his job in 1941 and retired with a gold watch in the 1970s. But as Taleb suggests, "The three biggest addictions are heroin, carbs, and a stable paycheck." Companies are not loyal. They don't care about you or me.

Another reason to have a plan B?

Unless you are working for an entrepreneurial company where you are learning transportable skills and being compensated in proportion to the value you bring, you are often at the narcissistic whims of your boss. The majority of people who leave their jobs cite "lack of appreciation"; that is, their boss hates them. Here she is, struggling to hold on to her job while all the young people are learning new skills, working longer hours, and with fewer responsibilities at home. She is afraid of you. She will block you from success and happiness. And she will throw you under the bus to save her own temporary status in the middle class.

Speaking of the middle class: average income for people ages twenty-five to thirty-four has been flat for thirty years. This is a shame because health care costs have skyrocketed and student loan debt (which specifically hits this age group the hardest) is up even more than health care costs. Corporations know that young people are forced to pay those huge student loan debts every month or the government will garnish wages. And since the rise of the internet, more jobs are automated, making corporations more efficient and less in need of human workers.

Bosses know this, workers know this, so this is how they keep wages down. It used to be young people who would start companies, be the innovators, and lead the forces of change for the generations to come. But no longer. The middle class is getting crunched. The way out is by diversifying passions, skills, the hierarchies one measures oneself in— and then as quickly as possible skipping the line so you aren't trapped by the rising costs in every area of life.

If that's not enough to convince you, consider this: two out of five employees in America blame their jobs for their gaining weight. They are sitting around all day, snacking, and too busy to take advantage of the wellness programs offered by their employers (63 percent say they don't use any of the employers' wellness programs). Spending on health care by employees *who are covered* by health insurance increased 44 percent between 2007 and 2016 according to the Health Care Cost Institute.

Why?

I have no idea. All I know is the end result: employees spend more money on health insurance with worse outcomes for their health. Jobs offer little comfort in good times, but as we all painfully learned during the Covid-19 pandemic and ensuing lockdown, a job offers no protection in a crisis—it doesn't save us from getting a deadly virus, it doesn't prefer our jobs, and, for all too many, it doesn't even provide enough health care benefits to fight a disease without the risk of personal bankruptcy.

A job won't protect you. What protects people is an ability to find new pursuits and new meaning in their lives, and to quickly get good enough at these new endeavors to provide for themselves and their families.

If you're still not sure whether you're ready to start experimenting with a plan B, ask yourself the following questions. If you land more on "yes" than "no," you have your answer.

- YES/NO: Will it improve my relationships with others?
- YES/NO: Will it improve my mastery of something I love?
- YES/NO: Will it increase my freedom and my ability to make more decisions for myself each day?

At a job, you are forced to be friends with people simply because they are in the cubicle next to you.

At a job, skill acquisition is limited to the particular micro-niche your company has assigned you to.

At a job, you have rules about what to wear, how to speak to the opposite sex, what time to come into work, what activity you have to do for fifty weeks of each year, and even what you are allowed to take home (don't steal the paper clips!).

A job will hardly meet the qualifications above. And those qualifications are the three components of what positive psychologists call "well-being."

So how do you get started?

TAKE BABY STEPS

Explore what side hustles are out there, investigate what your value might be to others, whether through the traditional job market or through contract work or by letting your curiosity or your hobbies lead you into new territory. Try different side hustles. Make an online course. Take a photography class, or a class on any subject that interests you. Is there anything you can consult on? Self-publish a book. Make YouTube videos about a topic you love.

By 1997, I was doing well enough with my side hustle building websites that I left my corporate job at HBO and started doing it full time. Then I scaled it into a business and eventually sold the business.

S. J. Scott writes books about habits and self-publishes them on Amazon. When he started, he was depressed, doing nothing, and sleeping on a couch. Now he makes up to $60,000 a month.

Hannah Dixon makes a full income as a virtual assistant while she travels around the world and writes about her experiences.

One friend of mine quit his job, wrote a diet newsletter called *What Would Jesus Eat?* (answer: essentially a Mediterranean diet), and now lives in a three-story penthouse in Medellín, Colombia. (Note: idea sex—the Bible + diets.)

The list of people I've spoken to who have left their jobs forever to do "gig economy" jobs is long . . . and getting longer.

Start small. Start easy. Don't get stressed about "building a business." Learn the skills, get one client, scale, repeat.

DIVERSIFY

Nobody can get rich from a job. You can't build real abundance.

As I mentioned before, the average multimillionaire has seven sources of income. This is important for two reasons:

1. A job is only *one* source of income. But if it's taking fifty hours a week (forty hours plus commuting, etc.) you won't have time for other sources.

> 2. Even more interesting, *being an entrepreneur* is only one source of income.

If you want to be an entrepreneur, go for it. You have a vision, you have a client, you have business sense, you have profits (so you don't need welfare from vulture capital firms), and you have a sense of how you can sell your company. But you can always expand the services you offer. One important thing to remember: your best new clients are your old clients. Meaning, if you want to make more money, don't try to get brand-new clients—try to provide more services or products to your old clients.

My friend Marvin, who has become a virtual assistant while he travels the world, has several clients for whom he books travel, makes restaurant reservations, keeps track of schedules, etc.

He wanted to provide a new service, so he called each of his current clients who were CEOs of companies and said to them, "You need to be more active on social media. Your competitors are all over social media." And they would say something like, "OK, but don't I need to hire an entire social media team?" And Marvin would say, "No. How about we start with me just posting two extra photos a day on your Instagram page? If you like it, we can figure out next steps."

One hundred percent of them said yes. He started doing that and charging each client about 50 percent more than he was charging them before. The clients who were happy asked for more posts, tweets, even articles that could be published on LinkedIn and Medium, so Marvin started writing those. In some cases, he would outsource these tasks to workers in India (for one-twentieth what he was making). In a few months he had doubled his income. He added a new title to his résumé: social media manager.

Then he added another service. One of his clients told him his dream was to meet Bruce Springsteen. Marvin said, "I'll make it happen." Marvin did his research and found a charity event where Springsteen was scheduled to perform. He told his client that he could arrange for him to attend the benefit but that he would have to charge for his "concierge services" instead of his typical fees as a personal assistant. The client said, "Of course!" Then Marvin called up all his other clients and asked them if they would like to go to a dinner with Bruce Springsteen. About half of them said yes, and Marvin said, "Great! But I have to charge my concierge fee instead of my usual assistant fee." They all said, "Of course!" Pretty soon Marvin was making about four times more per year than he had ever made before.

I know this story because I was one of those CEOs, and I later interviewed Marvin about it.

Another way to diversify is by expanding what I call your "status hierarchies." In a traditional job, titles and promotions are everything. I was jealous when my friend got promoted to senior programmer analyst. I was a junior programmer analyst, and I thought I was better than him. But he had been there longer. And then after that was assistant project manager, project manager, director, vice president, senior vice president, and then a bunch of other titles.

Everyone had a rank. Like in the military. And everyone had to pay respect to people higher in the ranking system. This sucks. We're not monkeys. But we are.

Every species of primate fires off neurochemicals depending on whether they are moving up or down the hierarchy of the tribe. The main benefit of being human is that we can be in more than one tribe. *We can diversify our status hierarchies.*

Money might be one hierarchy. Many people think net worth leads to more self-worth. For me, it was only when I was dead broke that I realized that self-worth leads to more net worth.

Golf score can be another status hierarchy. Or likes on Instagram. Or reviews on a creative project. Or skills acquired from an online learning site.

At a job, there is one hierarchy. Just like in a tribe of monkeys. But when you leave the job, you can pick and choose hierarchies.

Whenever I am feeling down about one area of my life, I focus on the areas of my life where I can improve, feel better about my status, and reenergize accordingly.

Happy brain chemicals like serotonin and dopamine (the leading causes of depression are when they are lacking) and oxytocin are all related to where you fit into your hierarchy. The way to not be a monkey and have more opportunities to increase your happy chemicals is to be in more than one tribe.

I used to day-trade. Day-trading is often horrible. You can lose money and every neurochemical is going the wrong way. But because I wasn't working forty hours a week, I had time to exercise (increasing endorphins, improving my stamina, etc.), I had time for creative projects (another status hierarchy), I had time to write and find places to publish my articles (seeding an alternative career for myself), or I could simply play chess more (improving my ranking in that world).

Diversification is not an "invest in stocks" strategy. It's an "invest in happiness" strategy. One that is harder when you have a full-time job.

TAKE BACK YOUR TIME

Most eight-hour jobs mean you work two hours a day *tops*. The rest of the day is spent sitting around in meetings, chatting with coworkers you don't like, taking coffee breaks, commuting, and doing nothing.

When I was at a corporate job, I'm guessing that the average person actually was working about 10 hours of the 40-hour workweek and mostly wasting time the other 30 hours. Thirty hours a week for 50 weeks is 1,500 hours. I wanted those 1,500 hours. Build a business, write a book, learn new skills, be with family, play games, whatever you want.

Being productive is not about sitting behind a desk so you get a promotion.

Being productive is about using time to make a better you.

CHAPTER 18

BECOME AN ENTREPRENEUR

I made a fool of myself in front of Tupac Shakur's mom.

Her manager said, "OK, show us what you got."

I sat down at his desk. His PC was off. I said, "How do you turn it on?"

"You don't know how to turn a computer on?"

"Well, I know how to turn an Apple on."

"Let me get this straight," he said. "You don't know how to turn a computer on and you want to do our websites?"

"Well, I do everything on an Apple." But he didn't hear me. He was laughing. I packed up my stuff. I was red in the face. I was afraid because it was a $90,000 job and I didn't know how I was going to make payroll.

When I walked down the hall, I still heard him laughing.

When I got back to the office, everyone crowded around and asked me, "How did the meeting go?"

"Great," I said.

One time I did a series of experiments. I made nine different websites at once and I wanted to see which one would gain the most traction. I created a website filled with IQ tests (people always seem to be obsessed with measuring their intelligence). I created various dating websites including . . . a dating website for smokers.

It didn't work.

Another time I started a company where we offered real estate agencies videos of all of the homes they were selling.

And another time I started a tea company. A rap label. A clothing line. A penny auction business.

And another time I started a debit card business before debit cards were a thing. I started a delivery company where we delivered from every restaurant in town. This was pre-web. I was the sales guy. I answered the phones. I made the deliveries.

I hated all of it. I wanted to write a novel. I was obsessed with what people thought of me. I wanted people to think of me as an artist.

I once asked Mark Cuban what passion he had that he then pursued so he could make money.

"Money," he said. "I was passionate about making a lot of money."

It's been thirty-four years since I started my first business. I've learned a little. I've seen billion-dollar-revenue businesses crash within days. I've seen the most unexpected businesses sell for hundreds of millions of dollars.

Business is really hard. It's hard to find a loophole in time and space that's big enough to fit money through.

I started my last business in 2015. We didn't take any investment. Last year it made $60 million in revenue.

I've sacrificed a life because of business. I was depressed for at least twelve years. My mom doesn't speak to me. My two sisters don't. I have no idea why they don't. I always feel I am nice to everyone, but maybe I'm just clueless.

In any case, I wish I had never started my first business. But I'm also glad I did.

Contradictions are fine. I wish I hadn't been so depressed for so long. I wish my older sister still spoke to me. I miss her.

Being an entrepreneur is going to shake your life.

You will go from the kind of person who gets a paycheck every two weeks to the kind of person who only eats what he kills. Don't worry. It will all be OK. But it will take you naked to the jungle, and you have to come out alive.

I haven't gotten a stable paycheck since 1997. Here are some lessons I've learned that will help you skip a lot of the mistakes that beginning entrepreneurs make.

SERVICE VS. PRODUCT

My first successful business was an agency. American Express was our first big client. They needed a website. This was 1995.

I was dirt poor. I shared a five-by-eight room with one other guy. We were kicked out when it turned out he wasn't paying the rent, even though I was paying him my share. American Express gave my company $250,000. It was just my brother-in-law and me, and we made the website and split the money. I wrote some software to help me. We made sixty thousand pages almost overnight. And I set it up so that they could check it and send notes to me on each page of the website. I didn't tell anyone about my software. I was afraid people would think I wasn't working so hard, because once the software was done, everything was easy.

What an idiot!

WordPress is software that helps businesses make websites. I basically made WordPress. WordPress is worth billions. Instead, I got my $250,000.

Products are always more valuable than services. I didn't know that then. I didn't know that software was scalable and so Wall Street valued it more. I thought, "They'll value profits and I will make less money if people knew how easy this was." I was wrong.

THE BEST NEW CUSTOMERS
ARE OLD CUSTOMERS

When I finished HBO's website, I moved on to the next entertainment company. I was always out there selling selling selling. I should've called HBO and said, "I think I can solve this software issue for you." I had already done a good job for them. I had many connections at all levels of the company. But once we finished the job I moved on.

Now I don't do this. Take my podcast. I'm not always looking for the best new famous guests. It's hard for me to find a great guest that I have rapport with, where I feel that instant friendship that is so rare for me. Now I know, if someone is a good old guest, then they are always welcome to come back and be a new guest.

Life is to be lived, not sold.

PEOPLE, PEOPLE, PEOPLE

A friend of mine was complaining about one of his potential business partners. "Jackie was supposed to be there to help out," he said. "She never even called to cancel. I'll give her one more chance."

I told him, "Why? Never ever call her again. People show you who they are right away."

"But maybe I can teach her. Train her."

"Did she ask you to be trained?"

"I know, I know," he said. "But it's good to give another chance?"

"Why?" I said.

"It just is."

No it isn't: 99.9999 percent of people never change. Maybe they aren't bad. Maybe they just don't have the same agendas as you and you're not meant to be working together.

One time I was doing due diligence on a company for a friend. They were the big buzz at that moment. They were the "Uber of food trucks." I heard a rumor that the partners were bickering a bit too much on phone calls with investors.

I said to my friend, "Don't invest."

He said, "Everyone loves the product."

"It won't work. If the two founders are arguing in front of strangers, imagine what they are thinking of each other when they go to sleep at night."

The company failed in six months.

People have an energy. I connect with you. You connect with me. And it's like we know each other. It's like we can complete each other's sentences.

Or not.

Not everyone has my values. Or my agenda. That's fine.

I had one boss, and I admired him so much. He was a hero, like a second father to me. And finally I worked for him. But every time we had dinner I would always feel bad afterward. Now I know. The gut is the only part of the body other than the brain that has neurochemicals (serotonin). If your gut says no, then listen to it. Otherwise you'll waste time, end up with an enemy, and lose money.

A business is made up of people. Your business will never fail because of the product. It will only fail if you have bad people.

OVERPROMISE AND OVERDELIVER

I get emails: "I have a correction for you. I think you meant 'underpromise.'"

No, underpromising is lying. Don't lie to your customers. Don't lie to anyone.

If I say I can get the job done in twenty days but I know I can do it in five, then I say five and deliver it in four.

First off, everyone else is lying and saying twenty. You win the job by saying the truth (five). And you push yourself and challenge yourself to do it in four.

You become a better person. The client is with you for life. And you exercise the muscle that pushes you to exceed your own expectations. Otherwise you're mediocre like everyone else.

Don't be mediocre.

EXECUTE FAST AND CHEAP

Don't waste time building a product at first. Get one person who wants to experience what you have to offer. Sell them your services (which will evolve into a product). Just get one customer. Execution of an idea *starts* with the customer, not with building the product.

The customer might pay for you to build the product, but an idea is not real until someone says, "Yes, I want it." Otherwise it might be a bad idea.

A business is an unlit match. Do whatever you can to light that match. Ignite the match and you'll see the world around you in a new light. The world that now has your business in it.

EXPERIMENT EVERY DAY

I started a social media business in the finance space. Every day we'd add new features.

I try a new thing for my business, my career, my creativity every single day. Like in science, most experiments don't work. Ninety-nine percent of them don't work. But when an experiment works, your life changes. If you never experiment, your life will never change.

I said yes to doing stand-up comedy. My life changed.

I said yes to buying ads in the back of New York City cabs.

That's right. I experimented by buying ads that ran on the passenger screens in New York City cabs. The ads featured a photograph of me holding a cup featuring the same photo of me. There were no slogans or taglines—the ads didn't point to any website or phone number. There was no call to action. There was no branding. I just wanted to see what would happen.

"Why are you doing this?" the people at the ad company said to me.

"It's an experiment."

"At least put a website address."

"That would ruin the experiment."

Anyone could put an ad in the back of a cab. But I wanted it to be so antipromotional that people would notice that and say, "What the heck is this? Who is this guy?" And if enough people wondered that, then perhaps it would get some media attention. Media attention = free advertising. And then more people would start to notice these strange ads. And then, when I finally did have something to promote—for instance, this book—I would be able to do that and have everyone's attention.

I don't know if the experiment will work. But I don't mind failing. And along the way, I'm learning. One person stopped me in the street and said, "Hey! You're that taxi guy! My eight-year-old loves you." And then he took a selfie with me and texted it to his eight-year-old.

In some ways, then, the experiment has already been a success.

BE A VOICE IN THE INDUSTRY

When I was building a venture capital business, I didn't want to be like the other ten thousand people trying to build a venture capital business.

I learned everything I could about the industry. I didn't have the right pedigree. I didn't have a Harvard MBA. I didn't work at Goldman Sachs and then start off as an intern at an older venture capital business.

So I read every book, listened to mentors, learned learned learned. And then I wrote about what I was learning. I wrote every single day. And soon people wanted to read what I was writing. I wrote for the *Wall Street Journal*, the *Financial Times*. I wrote books. It was hard to get people to listen to me at first. But I developed my own unique opinions; I became a voice that people wanted to listen to as an alternative to the normal BS that was on TV.

People became aware of me and wanted to hear about my business. And it grew and grew.

THE FUTURE IS RIGHT NOW

I think genomics is going to change the world. The health care you'll see in ten years won't be anything like the health care you experience now.

But the technology is not here yet. Maybe it's five years away. Maybe it's ten. And I'm not a geneticist. Or a scientist of any sort. So what? I'm not going to let things like "the technology doesn't exist" and "I have no qualifications" stop me.

There are plenty of ways to start a business right now:

- Start a hedge fund investing in early-stage companies. Or advise hedge funds on these companies (write a report).
- Write an industry newsletter about what you are seeing at cutting-edge conferences.
- Write a book about the technology. Start a podcast. Give a TED Talk about the future of genomics.

Don't complain. Don't say, "I'm not qualified." Don't say, "It's way in the future."

If you are passionate about something, you can find the business opportunities right now, and then you'll be first and you'll make a name for yourself.

DON'T SMOKE CRACK

I had a friend who was so excited about his business. He was a smart guy. A genius. He could always look at a business and tell me if it was going to work or not. Except for his own.

He had what I call "smoking crack bias." He smoked crack about his own idea. He thought it was great, and it was impossible to convince him otherwise.

Whenever I have a business, I ask myself every single day: Is this good? Why? What problem does it solve? Who really wants to pay for this?

This is a *real* bias, and 100 percent of people get it. You can only fight it as best you can, but you have to fight it.

LIST YOUR OPTIONS

So many people have an idea and then they think, "This is my business."

My approach is—you guessed it—to experiment with many ideas. Don't just start one business and throw everything you've got into it.

Don't waste one of your precious years devoting yourself to just one idea.

Walt Disney made some of the greatest animated films of all time. *Snow White and the Seven Dwarfs* and *Cinderella* are my favorite animated films. But Walt Disney made his first fortune on Mickey Mouse watches in the middle of the Great Depression. (See chapter 19: "The Spoke and Wheel (or How to Monetize Anything).")

List your options every day. Use the possibility muscle every day, ten ideas a day.

BUILD COMMUNITY

Start your email list right now. Always be in touch with the people who want to hear what you have to say.

Only talk when you have something unique to say. Otherwise, listen.

This was the most important advice I ever got about business. I started my list in 2012. This list is my friends, my family, my customers. It's the way I've made the most money.

But, most important, be around good people. The ideas are there.

But nobody is a self-made millionaire. Sometimes you need your superhero team in order to save the world. Rarely can you do it yourself.

CHAPTER 19

THE SPOKE AND WHEEL (OR HOW TO MONETIZE ANYTHING)

I never thought I would be able to make money from writing. If I had learned the "spoke and wheel method," maybe I would have been a little smarter with the various businesses I created and realized that there are many ways to make money off of a skill that you work hard at. I wrote every day for many years. I wrote for my blog, then I wrote for publications, then I wrote books, and so on.

I invested every day for years. First I made money day-trading, then trading for others, then investing in *other* traders, and so on.

Jeff Bezos sold books on Amazon. Then he sold clothes, then electronics, then food. Then he went "meta." He sold his logistics and shipping infrastructure and the Amazon Sellers program was born. Then he went meta again! He created Amazon Web Services, which allowed anyone to rent space and develop inside the enormous computer and cloud infrastructure he set up to run Amazon.

George Lucas made money from *Star Wars*. Then he made money from toys based on *Star Wars*. Then he made sequels. Then books spun out of *Star Wars*. Then comic books. Now the franchise (owned by Disney) is making money from spinoffs of the franchise (*The Man-dalorian*). And so on.

If you are making money (or expanding your audience, or creat-ing a brand, or creating art) but you aren't using the spoke and wheel method, you are losing out.

Your core idea is the wheel. From that wheel, there are many spokes. You can make money (or build brand, audience, whatever your goal is) with each spoke. For instance, let's say your core interest is in-vesting but you don't want to be a professional investor; rather, you want to create content about investing. What's the "wheel" and what are the "spokes"? If you don't use every spoke, you are leaving money on the table or you are missing an opportunity to build your brand and build a bigger platform. Investing is the wheel. What are the spokes? In this particular case, I'll describe the spokes and also ways to monetize them:

- Blog: Difficult to monetize. But you can potentially take your blog posts and syndicate them onto other platforms (LinkedIn, Medium, Huffington Post, Quora, investing websites, etc.) to build out your brand. These are the spokes to increase your brand with "blog" as the first spoke and "investing" as the wheel.
- Social media: Instagram, Facebook, TikTok, YouTube. You need huge audiences to monetize on each of these platforms, but these are good ways to connect to and interact with different audiences. If you don't interact with each of these platforms, you'll miss op-portunities to build more audience. That's OK. You don't need to be in touch with everyone, and not every audience is appropriate, but just being aware of that is important.

- Podcast: There are several ways to monetize a podcast. Imagine the podcast is now the wheel. Here are its spokes:

  a. Ads

  b. Sponsors

  c. Patreon (fans contribute to get extra content or other awards)

  d. Affiliate deals (also applies to blogs): You advertise for someone, give a special link to their product, and collect a fee if anyone goes from your podcast and buys.

- Email list: Offer a special report for free—all people have to do is sign up for your email list. Now they get, for free, all of your content no matter what medium you post it on. This way, your most interested readers get to consume your content without searching all over the internet for it.

These first four methods are more about the spokes used to build your brand, but they can be used for some monetization.

- Online course
- Online newsletter: If you price a newsletter (containing higher-value content than your free blog) at $20 a month and have two thousand subscribers, that's about $500,000 a year. If the spokes above are kicking in and you have an audience dedicated to your *authentic* and *unique* perspective, then two thousand subscribers for $20 a month is not a stretch. Ditto for the online course.
- For-pay Facebook group: I'm always impressed with how John Lee Dumas (host of the podcast *Entrepreneurs on Fire*) took his passion for podcasting and set up a great community on Facebook where podcasters can exchange notes, network with each other, ask questions, etc. He charges $2,000 to join the group and has 2,400 members.

- Merchandise: As you build a brand, you can make merchandise (a "This Day in Investing History" calendar, Warren Buffett T-shirts, mugs with stock symbols on them, etc.).
- Books
- TV show: A business model within the TV and film industry is to look at the most popular podcasts and buy television or film rights.
- Public speaking: As your authentic message grows in audience, you will be presented with opportunities to speak—first for free and then for pay.
- Consulting
- Starting or working for a hedge fund
- Day-trading

There's probably more. But with each category, and with each business idea, think of the idea as the wheel and start being creative by listing all the spokes that could be developed out of that wheel. Some of the spokes, like a podcast, can become their own wheel and have their own spokes for monetization and growth.

For example, Marie Kondo has her KonMari Method for tidying up. It's a specific approach to minimalism and it's unique to her. And while she has her very own unique take on minimalism and cleanliness, the KonMari Method is the result of idea sex: Shinto beliefs about cleanliness + the modern conception of minimalism. She's also an example of finding your purpose based on what inspired you when you were twelve to fifteen years old. When Kondo was that age, she gave up the chance to be class president; she preferred to be "bookshelf manager" because she was obsessed with tidying up everything in the class and organizing the books. And then she built on this obsession through idea sex: combining her interest in Shintoism with a more modern fascination with minimalism. Which makes sense. She spent five years as an attendant at a Shinto shrine. And when she was studying to be a sociology major at age nineteen, she started an organizing consulting business. In fact, her graduation thesis was on "tidying from the perspective of gender." The KonMari Method is her wheel. Some of its spokes are:

- Books: *The Life-Changing Magic of Tidying Up.* Millions of copies sold in more than thirty countries.
- TV: A Netflix show, *Tidying Up with Marie Kondo.*
- Email list
- Merchandise: She has a store where you can buy special blue light–blocker glasses, an organizer set known as Hikidashi Boxes, and many other items.
- Online courses: She offers a certification course so someone can be qualified to organize other people's homes using the KonMari Method. It's $2,000.
- Public speaking

While I'm sure she's made millions on her books and she probably did OK on her TV show (although not great; it's surprisingly hard to make money these days making a television show), where she probably makes the most money is her $2,000 certification course. One person who is familiar with the numbers mentioned to me she probably made more than $30 million on her certification course the year after her Netflix show came out.

If she had not done this method, she would have done OK. She has such a unique and powerful perspective, and she expresses it with the calmness you would expect from someone so engrossed in Shintoism.

Readers fell in love with her and her ideas and her books sold millions of copies. But by doing the spokes—public speaking, TV, merchandising, consulting, which led to her certification course—she has probably increased her net worth many times over.

The spoke and wheel approach is a great way to diversify your income stream so that you're not beholden to one single source of income—and no one person or organization or audience has the power to control you.

Despite the success of Kondo's book, let's say a publisher didn't feel like doing another one. No problem! She has TV. Then other social media. Then consulting. Then finally the online course. And all the spokes interconnect. Let's say she never got her TV show. No problem! She has her email list that she can market to.

Whatever your business ideas or interests are, write down (in one of the "ten ideas a day" sessions you use to exercise your possibility muscle) all the spokes that can emanate from those ideas and interests. You'll be surprised at how many opportunities you have out there and how easy it is to experiment with them.

For instance, Kondo doesn't have to make twelve TV episodes to get a Netflix deal. She has to write a proposal and have a few meetings. That's an easy experiment. She doesn't have to commit to a manufacturing facility to produce ten thousand Hikidashi Boxes for her store. Maybe she can put a photo of the box up before she makes a single one and experiment to see how many people order. If enough people order, she can place an order with a manufacturer and probably get a bulk discount. If not enough people order, she can cancel the orders she did get and return the money.

Everything can be tested with an experiment. There's no judgment. Some experiments will work and some will not. Nobody remembers what doesn't work. And what does work will help you build your brand, monetize your interests, and create more opportunities—wheels and spokes that you didn't initially realize were possible.

Nobody remembers that Walt Disney's first film company, Laugh-O-Gram, went bankrupt. Disney decided animation was the future and he went all in on it. He got investors, hired his friends, and made twelve-minute movies based on, wait for it . . . fairy tales. His cartoons were played at a local movie theater before the movies started. But it wasn't good enough. The income didn't cover costs, and despite it being the beginning of the Roaring Twenties, he threw in the towel and declared bankruptcy. His last movie for Laugh-O-Gram was a twelve-minute version of a little fairy tale called *Alice's Wonderland*. He immediately started a new film studio, this time named after himself, moved to Hollywood, and was trying to get someone to buy *Alice*. When an order came in, he convinced his best friend to move from Kansas City to Los Angeles, and then the magic started to happen.

Or did it? *Alice's Wonderland* was being developed into a series of cartoons, and Disney started work on a new series starring a cartoon . . . rodent. Disney's wife, Lillian, came up with the name Mickey Mouse, and when they first aired a cartoon starring this new lovable character, it totally flopped. Nobody cared. The Great Depression was coming. In October 1931, ten years after getting into the animation business and eight years after starting his second company (after surviving one bankruptcy), Walt Disney had a nervous breakdown. It's hard to pour your heart and soul into something and have every attempt fail. He just couldn't break even.

He was making good movies, even winning Academy Awards for short films, but Disney, the company, was struggling to survive. They were making commercials, short films, bigger films—the beginnings of a spoke and wheel technique—when finally one spoke shot up to save the company and propel Disney into history. They made a watch. In 1933, they put Mickey Mouse on a watch. In 1934, Disney sold a million watches at $3.75, saving the company and finally bringing in a profit. Walt Disney Productions was now the biggest watch company in the United States.

Of course, over the next few years, Disney added many spokes: full-length feature films, television programming, parks, books, more merchandising, etc. They started with that core idea—an animated cartoon character—and then added as many spokes as possible, but it was the one offbeat spoke, watches, that catapulted them to success. Now Disney is the biggest entertainment company in the world. But without the spoke and wheel approach, they would've failed.

CHAPTER 20

THREE WAYS TO MAKE A BILLION-DOLLAR BUSINESS

I wish I had read this chapter twenty-five years ago. But I guess I would've needed a time machine to do that. Because I'm writing this chapter today.

Think of those two neurochemicals in the brain that are devoted to pleasure and happiness: dopamine and serotonin. When I try to think of an idea that could make millions, or *billions*, I get excited with anticipation: maybe I can do this! And often I'll start something all excited, but eventually the excitement trails off and I lose interest.

The dopamine neurochemical has to transfer that excitement to the serotonin neurochemical. Serotonin is not fueled by anticipation. Serotonin is fueled by gratitude with what we have. Serotonin wants to further cement our bonds with the community and tribe. You feel happy when you provide service to others.

An idea starts as a seed in the brain. Anticipation and excitement water it. But as it grows, it must be loved and cared for. It needs our help to live. Service to others, service to our creativity, is the way to bring an idea into a fully developed business.

The three business models described in this chapter give me all sorts of exciting ideas when I think of how to apply them. But ultimately any good business is going to be about service to others. It's about providing great value to a community that you want to help. For so many years I tried business models with the end goal of making money, not of providing value. This is the wrong way to think about money. Money is a physical reward for providing service, just as serotonin is the brain's reward for providing value to a community.

Here are three business models you can experiment with until you find one that delivers the rewards—emotional and financial—you seek.

THE ACCESS ECONOMY MODEL

Let me ask you: What is your car doing while you are reading this? Is it in a parking lot? A driveway? Is someone else using it?

In 2000, Robin Chase realized that the average car was idle 55 percent of the time. A car might cost $50,000. It might be the most expensive item you own. And yet there are thousands of hours a year where it just sits around doing nothing. And even when I'm driving my car, the two seats in the back are probably idle, so most of the seats that I've paid for are idle.

What else is idle most of the time? If I own a home and my kids have grown up, then I might have rooms that are empty most of the time.

What if you came to me and said, "I would like to read *War and Peace*." I might say, "I've read it and it's just sitting on my bookshelf doing nothing. I'll lend it to you." That's sharing. If I say, "I'll lend it to you, but I'll charge you one dollar instead of the twenty dollars you might pay at the bookstore," then that's the "sharing economy." Or, as Robin Chase called it in her book *Peers Inc.*, the "access economy." Some people have excess, some people want access to that excess but don't know how to find it, and then there needs to be something in the middle that helps the two sides find each other, find the right price for giving access to the excess, handle customer service, security, etc.

The three parts of the access economy model are:

- Excess: Some people have an excessive amount of an item, call it X.
- Want: Some people want X.
- Platform: A platform in the middle helps people who want X discover it, buy it, transact securely, have customer service, deal with security, keep track of good customers and bad, etc.

So Robin Chase started the company Zipcar in 2000. Zipcar bought cars, so they had an excess of empty cars. Then there were people who wanted a car for short periods of time. The Zipcar platform used GPS to help people find empty cars, handled the financial transactions, dealt with security so that nobody stole the cars or damaged them, provided customer service, etc. In May 2000, two months after the internet bubble began to burst, Zipcar had its first car on the road. In 2013, Zipcar sold to Avis for $500 million.

When an idea is big, it doesn't matter if the country is in a recession, a depression, a booming economy, or some sloppy thing in the middle. In the access economy model, an idea is big if there are large amounts of excess and large amounts of people who want access to that excess. The access economy model is applied to many industries:

- Ride-Sharing—Uber: Some cars have an excess of empty seats. Some people want access to those empty seats to get from one location to another. But they don't want to drive the car themselves. They want to be picked up. Uber is the platform in the middle that connects the drivers with excess to the people who want access. It uses GPS to help the passengers and drivers find each other, and the platform sets the price, deals with customer service, makes sure the transaction is secure and the cars are reliable, etc. But why do I need a business to do that? In the middle of the day, there might not be cabs around and I might not be able to call a friend to pick me up. Before Uber, those were the only ways to "discover" a car that had empty seats that was willing to pick me up and take me where I want to go.
- Rental properties—Airbnb: Some people have empty houses. Others (for instance, families on vacation) might want to stay at an empty house instead of getting a bunch of hotel rooms. Airbnb is the platform that connects them.

The access economy model can even be applied to what are called "information products," like an online course or an online newsletter. Instead of access to physical objects, this version of the model provides access to excess knowledge.

Let's say a person knows a lot about knitting, including how to make money via knitting by creating stores on Etsy or elsewhere. They can create a course, "How to Get Better at Knitting and Then Make Money from Knitting." Then there might be people who love knitting and want to quit their jobs. An online-course company like Teachable or Coursera is the platform in the middle. I can go to Teachable and create a course on knitting, and now other people who want to make a living by learning how to knit better and then selling what they knit can search for my course using the platform in the middle (Teachable), which handles discovery, monetary transactions, customer service, etc.

When eBay started, people looked through their attics to see what valuable junk they had. They had excess junk they had been storing for years: books, antiques, clothes they no longer wore, etc. Other people might want this junk. eBay became the platform in the middle.

The access economy model creates an ecosystem of businesses:

- The platform itself: Uber, a transportation company, is worth billions without owning a single car. They simply provide the platform.
- The people with excess: Many people make a living by driving a car and finding the people who want their empty seats via platforms in the middle, like Uber and Lyft.
- The shovels and jeans people (see below).

In the gold rush, there was excess gold and there were people who wanted that gold. "Shovels and jeans" businesses were companies that popped up to help people maximize the benefits of the access economy model. People digging for gold needed to buy shovels. They needed to buy jeans. They needed banks to store the gold they found. They needed food and shelter in the locations where there was excess gold.

A modern version of this is the business of Airbnb managers. They find a bunch of people who are posting on Airbnb but might not be available to manage their houses. Maybe someone lives in a different country but owns an extra home in New York City so can't handle the day-to-day of managing it as an Airbnb home. So these Airbnb managers are in charge of photographing the homes so that they can maximize the number of people who want to stay in those homes, helping people check in to the homes, cleaning the homes, and managing the day-to-day of keeping up those homes in between uses.

Think about this:

> • What do you have excess knowledge about? And are there people who want access to that excess?
> • What items might have an imbalance between excess, people who want that excess, and ways for those people to find each other?

For instance, if I'm sick and can't leave my bed, is there a way I can find someone (a doctor or nurse) who can visit me at home without me having to go to the hospital? Maybe an "Uber for medical help" is a business model. I'm assuming this already exists but who knows?

Maybe someone with a medical degree doesn't want to deal with the headache of working full time for a hospital or starting their own practice and they'd rather use the Uber for medical help to find patients during the day and not have to pay the overhead that doctors with practices might have. This person would have excess medical skills and would need to join a platform that could help them find patients.

Another idea: a couple with three babies just moves into town and they don't know anyone. Now they want to go out to eat. Is there an Uber for babysitters?

A dating app like Tinder can be thought of as using the access economy model. Are there services you can provide that will help people either with excess or people who need access to some item? Ask yourself: What skills do I have that I can use to help those with excess maximize their potential in an access economy business?

One last thing about this model: there are two types of groups with excess.

There are companies that have excess (business to consumer). For instance, Zipcar was the only entity on the excess side of the business model. They bought or borrowed all of the cars that they rented out to people who wanted those excess cars.

There are also individuals with excess (consumer to consumer, or sometimes called "peer to peer"). After she left Zipcar, Robin Chase started Buzzcar, which took it one step further. Buzzcar allowed individuals to put their cars on the platform when the cars were empty (for instance, if a family went on vacation, they could make their cars rentable by listing them on the Buzzcar platform), then others could use the platform to find those now-rentable cars, and the Buzzcar platform would take care of everything else. Buzzcar was bought by Drivy in 2015, which was then bought by GetAround in 2019 for $300 million.

Sharing pays.

THE GOD ◆ HUMANS ◆ DATA MODEL

Two books I read had idea sex with each other.

They were Matt Ridley's *The Evolution of Everything* and Yuval Noah Harari's *Homo Deus*.

I was first exposed to Ridley's books when I read *The Rational Optimist*. It explains why people are always predicting the worst but innovation keeps solving all of the worst-case scenarios before they happen. In his next book, *The Evolution of Everything*, Ridley argues that it's not just humans that evolve but every aspect of life, and he proceeds to break it down, sector by sector.

In the book, Ridley discusses the evolution of marriage. When the structure of human groups evolved from nomadic hunter-gatherers to farmers and cities, marriage evolved from monogamy to polygamy, as men with the most resources started to marry many women. Women did this because it was better to be the ninth wife of an emperor than the only wife of a man who was going to starve.

However, this wasn't really a great deal for low-status men (or high-status women, who now had to compete for their husband's affections). So societies would go to war. Genghis Khan would invade a country; kill the men, children, and old women; and abduct the younger women to give more opportunities for his low-status men. Because polygamy, over time, led to an increase in violence, as societies became wealthier and wanted to focus more on innovation than conquest, polygamy evolved into monogamy.

And even now, the state of marriage is changing. Many couples choose to have common-law relationships (where the couple gains certain rights by virtue of how long they've been together rather than having an official ceremony). The average age of marriage is increasing. And there are fewer children per marriage.

Ridley goes on to describe how other aspects of our culture—cities, governments, entertainment, technology, etc.—all evolve over time. A great example is the art world. Art was initially prized based on how accurate it was to real life. Then art started to evolve and become more and more abstract. First impressionism, then Picasso's cubism, then Dali's surrealism, then Pollack's abstract art (which didn't seem to have any connection with reality), then Warhol's pop art (where the cultural impact of the item being painted became part of the art). Ridley's point: almost every aspect of life that we can think of evolves over time. And success in an industry follows the people who evolve with that industry.

Case in point: the computer industry in the 1980s evolved from the use of large mainframe computers that could power all the computational needs of businesses to smaller microcomputers that were becoming more powerful. My father was in the mainframe software business. He wrote software that would do the accounting for large companies on mainframe computers. "No large business is every going to be able to do all of their accounting on smaller computers. The Apple Macintosh is a toy," he told me in 1987. Two years later he was out of business.

Every industry on the planet is going to evolve (or has evolved) from a theistic approach to a humanist approach and ultimately to a data-driven approach.

I first came across Yuval Noah Harari in 2014 when taking his online course "A Brief History of Humankind" on Coursera. The book that course was based on, Sapiens, came out in English in 2015. In that book, he describes what he thinks the human of the future will look like. He also mentions a concept that stuck with me. It's the idea that every industry starts with a belief in God (or gods) as the expert, then humans, then data.

For instance, war: Two thousand years ago, if two kingdoms went to war, they might make sacrifices to their gods, have blessings from priests and shamans, and then send the men off to war. If the gods favored them, then they would win. If they had sinned against their gods, then there was fear they would lose. Even in the Bible, God is often the chief general of the Israelites, commanding Joshua to go into Canaan and conquer it. Or when God lost favor with the Jewish people, Israel would often be conquered. Eventually, the focus of battle transitioned to what the humans were up to: How many men on the ground? How many bullets? The field of military strategy was created by humans. And now, how is war fought? We use AI to target and kill enemies with drones from distances of thousands of miles. We use techniques in cybersecurity plus AI to scour enemy computers to hack into them and disrupt electric grids or get information. War is being fought every day over internet lines, and at any given moment there are millions or billions of "bots" scouring enemy computers to find holes and weaknesses and exploit them.

War went from theism to humanism to dataism.

Take medicine: Thousands of years ago, if you got sick, you'd often pray for help or go to your shaman to see if they could cure you with the help of whatever god you believed in. Fifty years ago, you'd go to your local doctor and he'd say, "Take two aspirin and call me in the morning." Now we sequence the genome of a disease, and we sequence the genome of a patient to determine what diseases they might be susceptible to. We use AI to analyze CT scans to determine if someone has cancer. We use AI and data to determine not only diagnosis but what medicines might be the best cures. We even use AI to help create the right chemical structures of medicines based on the chemical structures of the diseases the medicines are being developed to cure.

This can be applied to business models. In particular, money.

Look at the dollar bill. Our earliest beliefs about money are still carried over on the dollar bill. It says in the middle, "In God We Trust." Money is a story. If we believe in the story, then we believe that a simple piece of paper with drawings on it can be used in exchange for items like food, shelter, luxuries, and all of our needs. If we don't believe in that story, as has often happened (Germany in the 1920s, Zimbabwe in the 2000s, etc.), then the money of that country will collapse. So many countries throw everything they can into the construction of their paper currency to keep the faith of the people. The dollar bill has "In God We Trust" (theism). But just in case that doesn't do it for you, there is a picture of the first president, George Washington (humanism). But what if "In God We Trust" eventually becomes "In Data We Trust" and hence we are in the beginnings of an evolutionary change in money? Bitcoin is a test of this. Bitcoin is all data. Every "coin" is a program that ties into a massive database of what's called a blockchain that is shared by every "digital wallet" that can hold Bitcoins.

There is no physical representation of Bitcoin. The jury is still out on whether Bitcoin survives, but it's been around for more than a decade, over $200 billion worth of money is invested in it, millions of man-hours were devoted to its creation, and there have been plenty of opportunities for it to collapse (when countries tried to regulate it, when a pandemic occurred, etc.). And yet Bitcoin has managed to go up from ten cents to greater than $11,500 per coin at the time of this writing.

My point is that by understanding that industries evolve in this manner, we can look for opportunities in the gaps between these transitions. It's always worth asking: What industries or practices have not yet taken that final leap from humanism to dataism? And, given the eventual evolution of all things to dataism, what gaps in business models still exist and can be filled by our services or products? After Bitcoin was created, there eventually became a need for Bitcoin exchanges, then Bitcoin brokers, then programmers who could create applications on top of Bitcoin. In medicine, there are still many opportunities for the use of AI in diagnosis and treatment.

Now let's look at the world of dating: At first, people required their priests to arrange matches, then there were human matchmakers, and now algorithms on dating apps help you find the right match. Can this evolve further? What if when we all sequence our genomes, they're stored in a massive database? Will AI find that certain genomes have more successful marriages when paired with other genomes? Who will be the one to create this business?

What about law enforcement? Karma (what goes around comes around) came out of theism. But eventually there were human law enforcement agents (police officers) to handle the enforcement of laws.

And eventually, companies like Palantir started using data to predict potential criminal patterns (somewhat like the movie *Minority Report* where the police, portrayed by Tom Cruise, use data to predict crimes in the future). Palantir reviews bank transactions to determine suspicious, perhaps criminal behavior among a bank's customers.

Will the next step be to combine AI with GPS data to see what movements are out of character and perhaps criminal? Will algorithms running on the trends on Amazon sales rankings tell me which products I can develop quickly that will sell the best on Amazon? Will algorithms running on public data about housing prices, divorces filed in probate courts, and average life spans of an area tell me when real estate prices are about to go up (or down) or tell me the best time to make an offer at a substantial discount on a house that is about to be put up for sale?

We are just at the beginning (the first thirty years of what could be a thousand-year evolution) in the rise of dataism as a business model.

THE BOTTOM ONE-THIRD MODEL

Jim McKelvey, the co-founder of Square, told me, "Nobody wants to create a business serving the bottom third of an industry. Everyone competes for the top third. If you can find a business model that serves the bottom third, you could be the only player in the space, and that's worth billions." He should know.

Square helps small businesses accept credit cards. Credit card companies don't like to deal with small businesses—higher percentages of fraud, chargebacks, bankruptcies. Square assumes the risk of dealing with these smaller companies and acts as the middleman between the mom-and-pop stores that use Square and the major credit card companies and banks. The company started when Jim couldn't accept a $2,000 purchase for his glassblowing company because he wasn't able to accept credit cards. He partnered with Jack Dorsey, the co-founder of Twitter, and they created a card reader you can place on your iPhone to accept credit cards. They then convinced all the credit card companies to give them permission to offer credit card services to the tens of millions of small businesses that can't accept cards. Now, more than a decade later, Square powers the transactions for 40 percent of U.S. businesses, and the company has gone from just two people in a garage to being worth more than $23 billion.

There will always be industries that have a "bottom third" that aren't being catered to.

Amazon increased their book sales significantly when they allowed writers who weren't able to get a publisher to self-publish.

The rise of television was a way to provide entertainment for the many who couldn't afford to go to live outdoor entertainment. Even now, rather than spend thousands to go to the Super Bowl, you can watch it for free on TV.

As technology develops, there will always be ways to provide more services to people who were before considered unserviceable in a population.

For instance, there are millions of people who post YouTube videos but aren't in the top echelon of YouTubers who can charge for advertising on their videos. Is there a business model to help the bottom third of content creators? Is there a business model to help the bottom third of students who want to develop professional skills but can't afford to go to a college?

LegalZoom, now worth more than $2 billion (roughly; it's not public so it's hard to say), was created to help the tens of millions of people who can't afford common legal services, such as the writing of wills, divorces, simple contracts, etc. LegalZoom was started by a lawyer, Brian Lee, who has called himself "the worst lawyer ever." At one point, he was asked to draw up a simple document helping a business incorporate itself. The law firm he worked for charged $2,000. If you've ever incorporated a business, you know it's just a matter of filling out a form with the state and that's it. When he was told by his boss that the firm was charging $2,000, Brian said, "But it only took me twenty minutes." And that's when lightning hit. There was a huge gap between the cost of a simple legal service and the amount of labor he had to put into it. And with the internet, many of these functions or common services could be automated. He had no money, no business experience, but he knew that he could provide simple legal forms and services on the internet for almost no cost. And now, twenty years later, the company is worth more than $2 billion and he has since started the Honest Company, with Jessica Alba, worth more than $1 billion.

And when I write the "bottom third," I don't mean the "bottom third in wealth and income." It can be the bottom third in any industry.

For instance, in 2002, it still cost people tens of thousands of dollars if they wanted to make a relatively simple website. The creation of WordPress by Matt Mullenweg made it easy for the bottom third of people with technology skills (i.e., the people with zero to little tech skills) to be able to make a sophisticated website for free.

Ask: What sectors of the economy have only the top two-thirds being served?

☟ ☟ ☟

Understanding these three business models and their nuances will give you access to billions or even trillions of dollars' worth of opportunities.

Everywhere you see goods or services sold, ask: Who can't get these services and why? Is it people who would like access but don't know where to look? Is it an industry where better services could be provided if AI or data were more involved? Is it an industry where the bottom third is not getting properly served?

I wish I had fully understood these business models twenty-five years ago. But now I do. And I'm putting all three to use in my own businesses and investments.

CHAPTER 21

THE INCERTO TECHNIQUE

People think entrepreneurship or investing or switching careers is about being a risk-taker. I used to be a risk-taker. I'd take a risk and then I'd lose everything. I'd take a risk and lose money or reputation or friends or family.

When you are skipping the line, you are taking big risks. You are risking reputation. You are risking humiliation if you go too far too fast. You are risking failure, which is why your experiments have to be carefully constructed so their downside is limited. This is why it's important to have a set of skip-the-line strategies for reducing the risk of every high-stakes decision you make.

There are many books on risk, but there's one set of books I recommend. But I don't recommend you read the books. (The author probably won't like that I'm saying this, but: just read the titles and not the books. I mean, read the books if you want. But you just need the titles.)

The author is Nassim Nicholas Taleb and the books are *Fooled by Randomness*, *The Black Swan*, *Antifragile*, and *Skin in the Game*. Together, he calls this set of books his Incerto collection. Hence the name of this technique. *Incerto* is Latin for "uncertain." All life is filled with uncertainty, and often most of our lives are filled with attempts to create a false sense of certainty. But it is our ability to withstand the uncertainty and thrive from it that truly allows us to take a risk and to be able to handle the potential ramifications.

These titles describe four different skills—for making good decisions, for standing out in a crowd, for finding success in the spots people least expect, and for understanding the difference between luck and skill.

Again, the key to skipping the line is often to go to the room least crowded. These titles describe how to do it. And Taleb's track record suggests he knows what he's talking about. When the markets collapsed at the beginning of the pandemic, in February and March 2020, the hedge fund based on his principles went up 4,200 percent!

FOOLED BY RANDOMNESS

This is a reminder to wake up each morning and say, "I'm quite possibly the stupidest person ever." Not "definitely" but "quite possibly."

The first time I made money (and the second, and the third, etc.), I thought to myself, "I'm a genius!" and "If I can make it here, I can make it anywhere!" Sometimes if you massively succeed in one area of life, you think you can succeed in any areas. It's the "I must be a genius" feeling. I took it one step further. Not only was I a genius but I was done improving in life. I could clap my hands together, wipe them off, finished! Life was a good meal! Now I'm ready to just relax and enjoy.

This chemical concoction of false arrogance and false pride is the quickest way to failure. Notions of risk, skepticism, curiosity, and even mental health—they all fell away, even as I made blunder after blunder, always optimistically thinking all would be great at the end, and then it just never was.

I'm not complaining. I've done that enough.

When I sold that first business, I should have realized how much risk I actually took and how often I was saved by pure dumb luck—luck that the internet was the biggest investment bubble of all time. I had a tiny little company that made websites, and we sold the company for millions because a company that made burn gels wanted to get into the "dot-com" business to take advantage of the weird stock market boom that was happening for internet companies. It wasn't all luck. Making websites was the right industry to be in then. But the money part was luck. The fact that I sold to a burn gel company for stock and then that stock went from $2 a share to $48 a share in a year's time was dumb luck. The fact that I cashed out near the top was dumb luck.

And then, the dumb part, but not the luck part, is when I invested it all back into dot-com companies because I was an "internet genius." And then I kept borrowing more and more money to invest. Here I was, cashed out at the top (Luck? Skill? Unclear, since I had no reason to believe I had skill), and then I plowed it all back into the worst companies possible.

I was fooled by randomness.

Now whenever anyone shows me a good track record or a good outcome, I never assume they (or I) know what they are doing. I always ask: What were the risks? And did they succeed because they took those risks into account? Or did they succeed because they forgot about risk, got lucky, and success was the result?

Almost all the time, it's the latter.

THE BLACK SWAN

Black swans are rare. But they do exist. Taleb's point is that some things that seem statistically impossible (like an earthquake) happen much more than a normal statistical model would allow.

I'm going to be very simplistic. Basic probability theory was mostly developed to help figure out how to gamble on games of chance. If I take a modern coin and flip it a billion times, then about 50 percent of the time it will land on heads and about 50 percent of the time it will land on tails. It's possible, but unlikely, that it will come up heads a billion times in a row. If it does, then you can start to look for answers outside of probability, like that the coin might be weighted.

You can use statistics to help make betting decisions in games like coin flipping, poker, dice, even roulette. Using basic probability theory, guys like Ed Thorp created the science of card counting, which helped him take advantage of situations at a blackjack table when the odds were suddenly in his favor. If he simply knew the likelihood of a ten coming up next, and if that likelihood greatly changed during the game, then he could make large or small bets accordingly. (As a side note, in order to help him with counting the number of tens already used in a deck, he created the first wearable computer, which he attached to his shoe. He would tap his foot whenever a ten would appear and the computer would help with counting.) Thorp later took these same ideas and was the first person to apply them to the stock market, creating the field of quantitative investing.

Games are very controlled environments. When you flip a coin, there's no outcome other than heads or tails. And if the coin has balanced weight on both sides, then there really is a 50 percent chance that heads will come up. But as a system gets more complex, more "real life," it's not always possible to come up with the odds.

For instance, have you ever noticed that when someone is arrested for being a serial murderer, often the neighbors say, "That's impossible! He was such a nice boy"? Well, in all the days they knew him, by definition, he wasn't a serial murderer. So if you created a probability model of their neighbor being a serial murderer based on all the observations of the person, the odds would be almost zero.

It's like me saying, "I've been alive for 18,361 days in a row, so the odds of me dying are, best case, 1 in 18,361. It's almost impossible for me to die!" And yet, one day I will definitely die, defying all of the odds.

The "black swan" is the idea that if we look at the past and base all our decisions on prior observations, then most of the time we will make pretty good decisions. But we should always allow some room for the risks that could occur.

I don't know Nassim Taleb's investing strategies, but I imagine they work something like this: We know that the market has only crashed more than 10 percent in a single day on three days in the past hundred years. Any insurance model will look at those prior cases and say, "OK, so that's three times out of 25,000 days [a market year is roughly 250 days, with the market closed on weekends and some holidays], so the odds are 3/25,000." And then someone selling insurance to protect against a 10 percent down day will probably price such insurance very cheap since the odds are so astronomical.

But the fact that black swans exist means there are things we can't possibly predict, and that have not been modeled, that are risks in the market. So there are the known risks, which we've modeled to perfection, but we haven't also taken into account what happens if a small asteroid hits the planet and a hundred million people die. If you buy insurance on the market for huge shifts like 10 percent, you end up better by a tiny amount (and losing that amount) every month, but when the black swan event happens, you are up 4,000 percent, an amount that might be the equivalent of four hundred months of insurance even though you've only been paying for twenty months.

When I do any activity that is high stakes for me (starting a business, making an investment, even starting a relationship or trying a new interest or career), I always take into account the known risk (the CEO of the company I am investing in might die, I might die, the person I'm in a relationship with might be hiding massive debt from me) and act accordingly by reducing the size of investment or spending more time with the person to get a sense of what I might not know.

But then there are the black swans—the things I can't even predict or model since I've never had any experience with them.

So you have to think in terms of "insurance." When I start a business, my insurance might be that I have other benefits from starting the business (learning skills, making connections, etc.) that make it easy to pivot if the business doesn't work out. Or I might place a small investment in a competitor. If the business I am starting doesn't work, maybe it's because the competitor becomes the winner.

A relationship is hard to get insurance on. Which is why love is often the most painful risk of all.

ANTIFRAGILE

"You're so resilient," someone once said to me after I gave a talk. In my talks I always make fun of the different things that happened to me every time I went broke.

When you go broke, you lose most, if not all, of your friends. It's really true. You don't find out, as the cliché goes, who your real friends are. It turns out you didn't have any friends. Or, at the very least, those friends are taking a step back to see how things turn out. And it's hard to move forward if all you do is look back. Regret is a form of time travel. If I keep reliving the moments I lost everything, I can never escape the perpetual Groundhog Day I find myself in.

I have to have hope, something to latch on to that carries me into the next day with excitement and joy.

In the movie *Groundhog Day*, Bill Murray is able to move ahead in his life once he falls in love. At first he's bitter and resentful of what is happening to him. He becomes a worse person because of the bad event that is happening to him (the day repeating over and over). This shows his fragility. A bad and scary thing makes him even worse off than he was. This is the typical person in life. If a trauma happens, people often get some kind of post-traumatic stress that affects how they act when similar negative situations happen in the future. They become fragile and too weak to bounce back or live the life they wanted to live.

Look no further than some of our politicians, business leaders, and celebrities. The facade they spent decades building comes tumbling down and they aren't able to make a comeback. These are careers built on fragility. They're hard to maintain. Once a crystal vase is knocked to the floor, it shatters into a million pieces.

When I first went broke, I was so depressed I didn't think I could recover. I was a perfect example of fragility. It was only when I started exercising my possibility muscle and having a daily routine of health (physical, emotional, etc.) that I was able to start thinking ahead toward the future instead of maniacally obsessing over the past and all that I had done wrong.

Being "resilient" is when you bounce back to where you were but still make the same mistakes and have the potential for falling apart again. It's true. I was resilient. I kept failing, bouncing back, yet failing to learn my lesson, so I would fall to pieces again. You can bring all the pieces of the crystal vase to a . . . vase maker (I guess), and he can glue those pieces together. But if you still put the vase on the edge of the table and your dog likes to jump on the table, then you might be resilient, but you aren't really better off than you were before.

Being resilient is fine. And many people go through hard times, grit their teeth, and bare through to get to the other side.

Taleb's example of being "antifragile" goes one step further.

If something hurts you, it should make you stronger.

I didn't find what I would call real success until I started being openly vulnerable about all the mistakes I had made. I started blogging about them and built up a much bigger audience than I ever had just writing about financial topics. Being openly vulnerable and admitting my mistakes also forced me to learn lessons from them. I learned that if I don't write down ten ideas every day, I will quickly lose my ability to be creative. I learned that if I don't take into account risk in my activities, then it will be just as easy to fall apart again.

"If you do what you've always done, you'll get what you've always gotten" is a saying someone said at some point.

Antifragility is the essence of skipping the line. If you build up the skip-the-line techniques, it allows you to reach for higher and higher stakes, knowing that you have the ability not only to recover quickly from setbacks but to bounce back even stronger.

When I bomb doing stand-up, I'm able to look at the video (a form of insurance), see where I went wrong (often with the help of a more seasoned comedian), and try things that will improve the areas where I was weak (like doing stand-up on a subway to get better at performing in front of an unfriendly audience that needs to be instantly engaged).

After years of correctly analyzing companies but not correctly modeling for black swan events, I now structure my investments so that even if bad things happen, I'm diversified enough across a variety of investments that there's a good chance I'm properly placed to take advantage of any crisis that occurs. Not completely—because part of taking into account black swans is that you don't know what black swan will appear—but I'm protected enough to know that not only will I survive but I will flourish.

I asked Taleb this question: I haven't been to a medical doctor since I was a teenager. I'm afraid that I'm fragile, that the first time I get sick I'll just crumble in fear and anxiety. How can I be more antifragile? His answer was sort of like the idea behind vaccines: "Take a little bit of poison each day." I don't think he meant I should take cyanide. But it's the idea that is repeated throughout this book: You can't think your way to success. Nor can you think your way through every problem. You have to live with uncertainty, but you also have to *experience* and *do* the things you want to get good at.

Ask where in your life you would completely blow up and fail if an unbelievable occurrence happened and how you can get yourself to be a bit more antifragile now. What is the worst-case scenario and are you OK with it? And if you think you are OK with it, is there any way to mildly experience it and deal with it so you can see what your reaction is and then improve it?

When I was investing right after 9/11, I borrowed more and more money to invest while the market was going straight down. As a result, I went broke. And for many years I regretted it and didn't take chances (fragile), then for many years I built up my investing skills and would take chances again but then would blow it all again (resilient), but finally I am much more conservative and look more intently for opportunities with great upside and little downside that are unrelated to each other and unrelated to as many black swan events as I can think of. This has allowed me to be more antifragile. This is how you build yourself to being antifragile.

SKIN IN THE GAME

Having skin in the game means you have something to lose.

A journalist who makes a prediction that there could be an earthquake this year because there hasn't been an earthquake in a hundred years has no skin in the game. A year will go by and if the earthquake doesn't happen our journalist can say, "Well, thanks to my warning they took extra precautions." Or maybe nobody will even remember his prediction from a year ago and there's no consequences at all.

But what if he had to bet money on his prediction? And not just that prediction: What if he had to bet money on every prediction he made? Then the journalist would do more research, spend more time looking into where the fault lines are and how seismologists try to predict earthquakes. And, after all that, he might decide it's not worth the risk and he won't bet. And if he doesn't bet, he can't write about it.

That's skin in the game.

I love placing bets on "prediction markets." These are websites where you bet on the outcome of events like "Who will win the presidency?" or "Will Brexit happen by the end of 2020?" Sometimes I see a possible bet and I say to myself, "Oh, that will never happen." That would be enough to write an article. But if I have skin in the game (I have to make a bet), then I will do as much research as I can. I will become an expert.

Expertise is not built by taking classes and getting a certificate. You can't be a great soldier if you never go to war. You can't know what it's like to day-trade the markets and experience that horrible feeling of loss or that delicious feeling of success unless you actually trade the markets.

For every major decision, ask yourself: Am I going to lose something if this does not work out? It could be money. Or reputation. Or time. These are all disastrous things to lose. This is skin in the game.

Skin in the game will force you, in a very natural way, to do the research you need to do to reduce risk as much as you possibly can.

Understand that reducing risk to zero is not possible. Living with uncertainty is always part of skipping the line. Because the entire idea is that nobody has ever attempted to do what you are now doing. That is why success can be found there.

But taking on great perceived risk leads to the greatest reward. I say "perceived risk" because when you have skin in the game, you will privately reduce the risk by taking every action possible to do so.

CHAPTER 22

THE 30/150/
MILLIONS RULE

Another technique for skipping the line is to create a compelling vision and communicate it with others. If you can create a shared vision, you can build trust with others and you can accelerate collaboration and increase creativity. In the past few years, we've been forced to see our visions of the world shaken up and come close to being destroyed. Now more than ever, and for everything we do, we have to create a vision that links together our actions, our methods, our activities, and our reasons for doing things. Communicating that vision depends on understanding how communities form and influence each other.

The 30/150/Millions Rule took eighty thousand years to make, but it allowed humans to go from the middle of the food chain (eating just the bone marrow after a lion killed the prey and ate all the good meat and the vultures picked at the rest) to the top of the food chain (now the lion is in our zoos and the Neanderthals are all dead). The important thing about this rule is that it applies to leadership and organizations and where you fit within them as well as how to do well in an organization or business or industry or any kind of group.

Thirty: that's the number of people we can directly know. Nomadic tribes were thirty people. At this size, members of the community all know each other and they know which members of the tribe can be trusted. Jane knows Mike. Jane trusts Mike to go on a hunt. But when the size of a group exceeds thirty people, these bonds of trust and community start to break down. It's no longer possible to retain information about everyone, it's no longer possible to trust everyone, and the community starts to split into smaller groups again.

This dynamic worked just fine for about ten thousand years, but then around seventy thousand years ago, humans developed an important skill that no other animal had, not even other near humans like Neanderthals: gossip. Now Jane could say to Harry, "Mike is good to hunt with," and now Harry, who trusts Jane's judgment, had confidence he could hunt with Mike, even if Mike was a total stranger. *Bam!* It's the end of Neanderthals and every other type of *sapiens* except for humans. Go team!

This works in groups up to about 150 people. We can retain information and gossip about roughly 150 people. If we don't have 150 people to gossip about, then we feel the need to read gossip magazines and follow social media influencers to keep up with people like Kim Kardashian and Barack Obama, etc. This rule applies to businesses too. When the number of employees is between 30 and 150, the use of internal newsletters, awards, and specific job titles helps make the organization run smoothly. Here a little bit of hierarchy goes a long way. Since we can't possibly know everyone personally, we need other ways to assess their reliability—whether we can trust them.

But what really helped humans rise to the top of the food chain—to skip the line in evolutionary terms—took place about ten thousand years ago. It's a tool that enabled complete strangers, living thousands of miles apart, to work together: stories.

If you tell a good story and two people from opposite sides of the world trust that story, then they can work together. Hence religion. Hence politics. Hence labels.

If you are "pro-choice" and I am "pro-choice," then we get a sense that we can work together. If you label yourself "Republican" and I label myself "Republican," then we get a sense we can work together. This is because we share the same "story" of how the world works and our place in it. Nationalism is a powerful story. Political dividing lines like the environment, pro-choice/pro-life, etc. are powerful stories. Religions are powerful stories that unify millions of people. All of these stories allow us to work with strangers with whom we have nothing else in common. Oh! You drive a Honda Civic? Me too! Now maybe we can work together. (Actually, I am banned from driving, but this is just an example.)

What are the components of a good story? And are you the hero of your story?

As outlined by Joseph Campbell in *The Hero's Journey*, the "arc of the hero" roughly has:

- A reluctant hero: Luke Skywalker wanted to go to other planets but felt obligated to stay on his uncle's farm.
- A call to action: Peter Parker's uncle is killed in front of him and he realizes he could have stopped the murder if he had used his powers.
- A journey: We meet new friends, and we encounter bigger and bigger problems. Buddha meets the initial monks who want to be his disciples and warring nations are constantly trying to disrupt the peace he has created in his grove.
- A final encounter with the biggest problem of all and the defeat of it: Luke Skywalker destroys the Death Star.
- A return home to tell the tale.

A brand is a powerful story. If you can craft a story about your product or service that connects with others, you're in business. This was shown in a recent study where a guy bought a bunch of junk and then sold it on eBay. He made x dollars. Then he sold duplicates of the same items on eBay but told a story about where each product came from, why it was important, etc. They were still the same products, but he made x dollars × 4. Stories create value and allow us to cooperate with millions of strangers. The only problem is we've been evolving for millions of years and this has only been in our genes for ten thousand years. So occasionally it breaks down. Hence wars, hence financial crises, etc.

Being aware of the stories in my life helps me to decide what is BS and what is something that is really true to me. The only way to tell if a story is true is the way I feel inside. When I laugh, that is real to me. When I feel good, that is real to me. When I am kind to people, regardless of their story, this makes me feel better. But I will never argue with someone about a story. I only have so much energy and I like to use it as efficiently as possible so I can love my family, create things, do fun things, and be healthy.

I am a personal energy minimalist.

CHAPTER 23

WHAT TO TELL YOUR KIDS (OR 10+ RULES FOR LIVING A GOOD LIFE)

I didn't want to have kids. Ever.

But then I had one.

She moved in. A one-foot-tall new U.S. citizen who didn't speak English, cried all the time, shat on the floor, and sucked on my wife's breasts whenever she wanted to.

Still, I put up with her. And I loved her more than I had loved anyone ever. More than I loved at least seven billion other people on the planet.

She turned twenty the other day. *Twen-ty!*

I don't know if she listens to my advice, but here are some of the things I wrote to her about how to try to live a good life. Or at least to not live the life of worry, pain, fear, and anxiety that I lived.

A funny thing happened on the way to her going from age zero to age twenty. I had another kid. I never thought I could love someone as much as I loved my first child. But I was wrong. My love for both of them increased. And then I got married and my wife, Robyn, had three kids. All three are about the same age as my children. Four daughters and a son. I love all of them. Josie, John, Sarah, Lily, Mollie, in order of age. Every day, all five children (and now mini-adults) have a new set of problems. And they want to tell you these problems. They are very *important*!

The key is not to respond. They very rarely want advice. They very rarely listen to advice. They watch though. They watch your every move. To be a good parent, you have to be a good person. You have to demonstrate the right way to live, not tell them the right way to live.

But also, I'm a pushover. They know who to ask permission from. My wife says, "No!" and I say, "Yes. But ask your mom!"

They don't listen to my advice. So I try to live by example:

1. Always go to the place least crowded.

    Success is found where nobody else is.

    A friend of mine's daughter wanted to get into Harvard. But how many kids in the New York City area with good grades and good SAT scores apply to Harvard? All of them. There's too much competition. She got fascinated with race car driving and took lessons as soon as she was old enough. She was passionate about it. She watched videos and got on the racetrack with a coach whenever she could. And eventually she did OK in races. Not a winner but good enough. Good enough at car racing made her the *only* teenage female professional race car driver applying to Harvard. She got in. But she was having so much fun doing what she loved (and getting sponsorships along the way) that she turned Harvard down to pursue her dream.

    Another way to put this comes from my favorite quote

from Kevin Kelly, the founding editor of *Wired* magazine: "Don't be the *best*, be the *only*."

2. Being secretly good to people = superhero. Being famous for the sake of being famous = loser.

3. Good relationships = good life. Bad relationships = bad life.

Similar to this: Audience selection is better than audience development. You don't want people around you who you always have to teach.

World-champion-level chess players often travel with a "second." That's a person who will help them analyze positions, come up with new ideas to try in important matches, study the opponents games and try to guess what they will play, and so on. The second of a world-champion-level player is usually another player in the top ten in the world, maybe even a former world champion. Bobby Fischer, the world chess champion in 1972, was once asked, "Why don't you have a second?" He said, "I don't like to give chess lessons in the middle of an important match."

This might have been a bit over the top, but the point is: select the right people so you don't have to waste time developing them. Take your time to select the right people to be around you, to be your team. Don't select people who you then have to develop.

4. If you do what you've always done, you'll get what you've always gotten.

If you want your life to change, do something different, something unexpected. Take a wrong turn off a dirt road.

Exercise the possibility muscle. Every day write down ten ideas. You will see more possibilities than ever to do things differently.

5. Sleep and rest.

    People always say, "Work hard. Work a lot. Hustle and grind." But you're only going to grow when you rest. Working is when you do things. Resting is when the brain grows and rewires itself. Put it in your online calendar: twenty minutes in the morning and twenty minutes in the afternoon where you put the phone down, pause the computer, daydream, or just take a walk.

6. Bad things will happen. Treat them like opportunities.

    You are going to have to repeat that every day.

7. Don't feel sorry for yourself ever. See above.

8. Be creative every day.

    Everyone else will stay in their lane. But if you are creative every day, you'll get further and faster than everyone else.

9. Live life as if today might be your last day.

    It might not! So don't kill people you hate. But don't do something today in hopes of a better outcome tomorrow. Make the most of each day.

10. *Hara hachi bun me.*

    Okinawa, Japan, has the highest percentage of centenarians in the world. And these centenarians aren't sick in bed. Okinawa also has one of the highest percentage of people over one hundred years old with high quality of life. In Okinawa they practice a philosophy called *hara hachi bun me*, which means "eat 80 percent of your capacity." Because people only realize they are full about twenty minutes after they are full (the signals for "full" travel slowly from the stomach to the brain), you need to get a sense of how long it takes you to be full. And at 80 percent of that point, stop.

I mean, enjoy your food. But always remember that even when you feel hungry, you aren't starving. In the U.S., you live in a country where most people are full every day. If you eat more, then you'll be unhappy. And if you want to live to a rich old age with high quality of life, this is a good philosophy to follow.

Those are the ten things. Here's a bonus thirteen:

1. READ!

    You are so lucky. Most people don't read. Those people are losers. If you read one good thing a day, then in a few years you'll know thousands more things than anyone else.

2. Don't "can't."

    Don't ever say you "can't" do something. If there's something you passionately want, there's always some way to get it or get close to it.

3. Double-park with impunity.

    If you have to get somewhere, don't be afraid to

double-park. At the first chance, though, get someone to move your car. Don't be a dick.

4. Buy convenience.

If you have to spend your last dollar to have an easier commute, always do it. Convenience is worth more than material possessions.

5. Don't read the news.

Every second you read "news," you could be reading or doing something that can improve your life.

People who write news are phonies. I was once backstage at a prominent news show that I often appeared on. The producer was generous in spending time with me and explaining how everything worked. But the most important thing he said to me was "Everything we are doing here is to get us from one ad spot to the next." And that sums up why you shouldn't read the news. (See "The Attention Diet" section in chapter 13: "Microskills Everyone Should Learn" for answers to the questions that come up when I suggest this.)

6. Everything worthwhile requires skill.

If you want to achieve something, you need more skill than all of the other people trying to achieve it. Break apart a skill into twenty microskills. Figure out how, each day, you can get better at each microskill. Don't worry about the outcomes. Outcomes happen naturally as you build the skills. Just focus every day on improving a tiny, tiny bit.

7. If someone doesn't like you, then ignore them.

   This seems obvious but it isn't. Sometimes when someone doesn't like me, I waste time trying to get them to like me. This is how you win the loser's trophy.

8. It doesn't mean anything to "be yourself."

   But still, decide every day what you believe in and don't compromise on those beliefs. Every time you compromise, you become part of the machine. Much more happiness is found outside of the machine.

9. Don't believe something just because everyone else believes it.

10. Don't outsource self-esteem.

   When you love someone, don't depend on them for self-esteem. It's hard enough for the other person to have self-esteem, let alone help you have self-esteem.

   Limit the number of people you look to for validation. Even if you value someone else's opinion, never forget that there will be times when their opinion will not be right for you; it's only right for what they want in the world.

   Maybe even those closest to you don't want you to skip the line. Maybe they are afraid you are about to take off on a rocket ship and leave them behind. This could be a valid concern for them. It doesn't mean they are bad and you should ignore what they say. But be aware of their agenda. Everyone has an agenda.

11. Facts are irrelevant.

People sometimes say to me, "Why is the stock market going up today? There was bad news!"

It's because facts are not important. We never see the full picture in any situation. Every situation between people is complex. There are multiple stories, and facts to one person are opinions to another. What people care about are certainty and uncertainty. The stock market is a barometer of people's perception of the level of uncertainty in the world. More uncertainty, more panic; more certainty, less panic.

Facts aren't as useful as possibilities.

12. There's always a good reason and a real reason.

I remember when you once told me you had to go study in the library. I asked why. You said that all the books you needed were there and you couldn't do the research online.

That was a good reason. I couldn't argue with it. But you forgot to mention that there would be boys at the library and you wanted to see them. That was a real reason.

When someone gives you a good reason, a reason that is impossible to argue with, it might be true and important. But always ask what the real reason is. There is always a real reason.

13. Don't forget to call me.

I love you.

ACKNOWLEDGMENTS

In chronological order of birth, my children:

  Mollie Altucher

  Lily Samuels

  Sarah Samuels

  John Samuels

  Josie Altucher

Some of you are old family, some of you new. "Acknowledgments" is the wrong name for this section. Yes, I acknowledge you. But, perhaps more accurate, this book is written for you.

This book is not advice a researcher discovered in a social psychology laboratory. This is advice hard earned from my own experiences and the experiences of thousands of others I have spoken to or studied.

I hope you all discover many different passions throughout your lives, change careers and interests dozens of times, and always do things where your heart and mind are saying the same thing.

This book, I hope, can help you skip the line so you can feel the pleasure of being the best at whatever it is you want to be.

I would also like to acknowledge the many people who have shared their knowledge on my podcast. Selfishly, I have asked all of you on not to spread your message or ideas (although that happened) but so that I could be a better person. And in this book I share many of your ideas alongside my own stories.

Aaron Berg	Bill Beteet
Aaron Carroll	Bill Cartwright
Adam Grant	Bill Glaser
Adam Perlman	Blake Hutchison
A. J. Jacobs	Blake Mycoskie
Alex Berenson	Bo Eason
Alex Blumberg	Bobby Casey
Alex Lieberman	Bobby Hundreds
Allison Task	Bonnie McFarlane
Amanda Cerny	Brad Meltzer
Amy Koppelman	Brad Thor
Amy Morin	Brandon Webb
Anders Ericsson	Brendon Lemon
Andrew Huberman	Brett McKay
Andrew Schulz	Brian Keating
Andrew Yang	Brian Koppelman
Annie Duke	Brian Scott McFadden
Anthony Ervin	Byron Allen
Arianna Huffington	Cal Fussman
Ashlee Vance	Cal Newport
Aubrey Marcus	Caleb Carr
Barbara Corcoran	Carl Allen
Barry Michels	Caroline Hirsch
Bassem Youssef	Cass Sunstein
Ben Mezrich	Charlamagne Tha God
Bert Kreischer	Charles Duhigg
Beth Comstock	Charlie Hoehn

Chase Jarvis

Chelsea Handler

Cheryl Richardson

Chief Don DeLuca

Chip Conley

Chris Anderson

Chris Brogan

Chris Distefano

Chris Gethard

Chris Smith

Chris Tucker

Chris Turner

Chris Voss

Chuck Klosterman

Chuck Palahniuk

Craig Benzine

Dan Ariely

Dan Carlin

Dan Harris

Dan Lyons

Dan Roth

Dan Schawbel

Dani Zoldan

Danica Patrick

Dante Nero

Dave Asprey

Dave Barry

David Bach

David Epstein

David Goggins

David Kwong

David Litt

David McCandless

David Rubenstein

David Sinclair

Daymond John

Dean Graziosi

Debbie Millman

Dennis Woodside

Derek Sivers

Don McLean

Doug Casey

Dov Davidoff

Dr. Oz

Dr. Sanjiv Chopra

Dr. Steven Gundry

Eddie Ibanez

Elizabeth Smart

Ellen Fein

Eric Adams

Eric Schmidt

Eric Weinstein

Erika Ender

Evan Carmichael

Farnoosh Torabi

Floyd Landis

Frank Oz

Frank Shamrock

Fred Stoller

Gabriel Weinberg

Gabrielle Bernstein

Garry Kasparov

Gary Gulman

Gary Vaynerchuk

Geno Bisconte

George Gilder

Gilbert Gottfried

Godfrey

Gregory Zuckerman

Gretchen Rubin

Griffin Dunne

Hal Elrod

Heather Monahan

Henry Winkler

Howard Marks

Hugh Howey

Humble the Poet

Jack Perry

Jackie Martling

Jairek Robbins

James Frey

Jamie Kilstein

Jamie Metzl

Jamie Wheal

Jason Calacanis

Jason Feifer

Jay Shetty

Jay Wujun Yow

Jeannie Gaffigan

Jeff Garlin

Jeff Goins

Jen Sincero

Jennifer Shahade

Jenny Blake

Jesse Itzler

Jessica Banks

Jewel

Jim Cramer

Jim Kwik

Jim McKelvey

Jim Norton

Jimmy O. Yang

Jocko Willink

Joe De Sena

Joe Moglia

Joey Coleman

John C. McGinley

John Mackey

John Maxwell

John McAfee

John McCaskill

John Paul DeJoria

John Phillips

Jon Alpert

Jon Macks

Jon Morrow

Jon Ronson

Jonah Berger

Jonathan Kay

Jordan B. Peterson

Jordan Harbinger

Jordan Shlain

Joseph "Rev Run" Simmons

Joshua Foer

Joule Financial

Julia Cameron

Justice Sonia Sotomayor

Kai-Fu Lee

Kamal Ravikant

Kareem Abdul-Jabbar

Keith Hernandez

Kellan Lutz

Ken Follett

Ken Langone

Kevin Allocca

Kevin Kelly

Kevin Surace

Lewis Howes

Linda Papadopoulos

Loretta Breuning

Lori Gottlieb

Marc Ecko

Marc Lore

Marcus Lemonis

Maria Konnikova

Maria Menounos

Mark Cuban

Mark Divine

Mark Malkoff

Mark Manson

Marty Makary

Matt Clayton

Matt Mullenweg

Matt Ridley

Matthew Berry

Michael Ovitz

Michael Singer

Michio Kaku

Mike Bullard

Mike Love

Mike Massimino

Mike Posner

Mike Reiss

Mike Rowe

Mike Van Cleave

Nancy Cartwright

Nas

Nassim Nicholas Taleb

Nathan Rosborough

Neil deGrasse Tyson

Neil Strauss

Nell Scovell

Nicole Lapin

Nik Wallenda

Noah Kagan

Noam Dworman

Ozan Varol

Paul Mecurio

Paul Oyer

Paul Reiser

Paul Shaffer

Pete Holmes

Peter Diamandis

Peter Openshaw

Peter Thiel

Phillip Stutts

P. J. O'Rourke

Ramit Sethi

Randall Stutman

Ray Dalio

Ray J

Rich Cohen

Rich Karlgaard

Rich Roll

Richard Branson

Rob Corddry

Robert Cialdini

Robert Greene

Robert Kurson

Robyn Altucher

Roger McNamee

Ron Paul

Roy Niederhoffer

R. P. Eddy

Ryan Deiss

Ryan Holiday

Sachit Gupta

Sam Harris

Sam Parr

Sara Blakely

Sasha Cohen

Scot Cohen

Scott Adams

Scott Barry Kaufman

Scott Galloway

Scott Steindorff

Scott Young

Sean Kim

Sebastian Maniscalco

Seth Godin

Shane Snow

Shawn Stevenson

Sheila Nevins

Sherri Schneider

Sherrod Small

Spike Cohen

Stephen Dubner

Stephen Merchant

Stephen Tobolowsky

Steve Case

Steve Cohen

Steve Scott

Steven Johnson

Steven Kotler

Steven Pressfield

Steven Schwarzman

Susan David

Susie Essman

Tank Sinatra

T. D. Jakes

Tero Isokauppila

Terry George

Tiffany Haddish

Tim Dillon

Tim Ferriss

Tim Kennedy

Tim Larkin

Tim Ryan

Tim Staples

Tionne "T-Boz" Watkins

T. J. Miller

Todd Barry

Todd Herman

Tom Bilyeu

Tom Papa

Tom Quiggin

Tom Rath

Tom Shadyac

Tony Hawk

Tony Robbins

Tony Rock

Tucker Max

Turney Duff

Tyler Cowen

Tyra Banks

Wally Green

Wayne Baker

Wayne Dyer

Will Shortz

William Shatner

Wolfgang Puck

Wyclef Jean

Wynton Marsalis

Yancey Strickler

Yannis Pappas

Ylon Schwartz

Yuval Noah Harari

Zuby

And I'm extremely grateful to the many people who helped me with this book, but, in particular, this would never have seen the light of day without the amazing efforts of Suzanne Gluck from WME and Hollis Heimbouch from HarperCollins. It's always a pleasure to work with people who are the best at what they do.

ABOUT THE AUTHOR

James Altucher is an entrepreneur, active angel investor, writer, podcaster, stand-up comedian, and chess master. He has started and run more than twenty companies and invested in over thirty. He is the author of eighteen books, including the bestsellers *The Power of No* and *Choose Yourself!* His writing has appeared in the *Wall Street Journal*, the *Observer*, *Financial Times*, HuffPost, and TechCrunch. He also writes a popular blog and hosts a successful podcast, *The James Altucher Show*, that has had more than 80,000,000 downloads. An eight-episode docuseries based on his book *Choose Yourself!* was released on Amazon in 2020.